Onward Christian Soldiers?

Dilemmas in American Politics

Series Editor   **L. Sandy Maisel,** *Colby College*

Dilemmas in American Politics offers teachers and students a series of quality books on timely topics and key institutions in American government. Each text will examine a "real world" dilemma and will be structured to cover the historical, theoretical, policy relevant, and future dimensions of its subject.

BOOKS IN THIS SERIES

Onward Christian Soldiers? The Religious Right in American Politics, Second Edition, Clyde Wilcox

To Serve God and Mammon: Church-State Relations in American Politics, Ted G. Jelen

Money Rules: Financing Elections in America, Anthony Gierzynski

The Accidental System: Health Care Policy in America, Michael D. Reagan

The Dysfunctional Congress? The Individual Roots of an Institutional Dilemma, Kenneth R. Mayer and David T. Canon

The Image-Is-Everything Presidency: Dilemma in American Leadership, Richard W. Waterman, Robert Wright, and Gilbert St. Clair

Checks and Balances? How A Parliamentary System Could Change American Politics, Paul Christopher Manuel and Anne Marie Cammisa

"Can We All Get Along?" Racial and Ethnic Minorities in American Politics, Second Edition, Updated, Paula D. McClain and Joseph Stewart Jr.

From Rhetoric to Reform? Welfare Policy in American Politics, Anne Marie Cammisa

Two Parties—Or More? The American Party System, John F. Bibby and L. Sandy Maisel

Making Americans, Remaking America: Immigration and Immigrant Policy, Louis DeSipio and Rodolfo de la Garza

The New Citizenship: Unconventional Politics, Activism, and Service, Craig A. Rimmerman

The Angry American: How Voter Rage Is Changing the Nation, Second Edition, Susan J. Tolchin

No Neutral Ground? Abortion Politics in an Age of Absolutes, Karen O'Connor

Payment Due: A Nation in Debt, a Generation in Trouble,
Timothy J. Penny and Steven E. Schier

Bucking the Deficit: Economic Policymaking in the United States
G. Calvin Mackenzie and Saranna Thornton

Remote and Controlled: Media Politics in a Cynical Age, Second Edition
Matthew Robert Kerbel

Onward Christian Soldiers?

The Religious Right in American Politics

SECOND EDITION

Clyde Wilcox
Georgetown University

Westview Press
A Member of the Perseus Books Group

Dilemmas in American Politics

Published in 2000 in the United States of America by Westview Press, 5500 Central Avenue, Boulder, Colorado 80301-2877, and in the United Kingdom by Westview Press, 12 Hid's Copse Road, Cumnor Hill, Oxford OX2 9JJ

Visit us on the World Wide Web at www.westviewpress.com

Library of Congress Cataloging-in-Publication Data
Wilcox, Clyde, 1953–
    Onward Christian soldiers? : the religious right in American politics /
Clyde Wilcox.—2nd ed.
       p.   cm.—(Dilemmas in American politics)
    Includes bibliographical references and index.
    ISBN 0-8133-9759-6
    1. Christianity and politics—United States—History—20th century.   2. Conservatism—
Religious aspects—Christianity—History—20th century.   3. Conservatism—United States—
History—20th century.   4. United States—Politics and government—1945–1989.
5. United States—Politics and government—1989– .   6. United States—Church history—
20th century.   I. Title.   II. Series.

BR526 .W53   2000
320.5'5'0973—dc21

                                                                                              00-040817

The paper used in this publication meets the requirements of the American National Standard for Permanence of Paper for Printed Library Materials Z39.48–1984.

10   9   8   7   6   5   4   3   2   1

In memory of Grace Ice, Beulah Musgrove, and Zoe Wilcox, three sisters who made me think, made me laugh, and made me work

Contents

4 Assessing the Christian Right   97

5 The Future of the Christian Right   133

Illustrations

Tables

Figures

Photos

Boxes

Maps

Preface

Writing about the Christian Right always brings out the schizophrenic elements in me, as my roots war with my politics. I grew up in rural West Virginia, and many of my family and friends who still live in that area are supporters of the Christian Right. My father was a fundamentalist Sunday school teacher who taught me the Bible and was a fan of Jerry Falwell. My mother was a charismatic who regularly watched Pat Robertson's *700 Club* and who greatly enjoyed a Spirit-filled religious retreat every spring. My great-aunts, to whom this book is dedicated, seldom missed a televised sermon by Charles Stanley.

As a child I attended the Walnut Grove United Methodist Church, a church in the revivalist tradition of Spirit-filled fundamentalism. I was often drafted to play the piano in revival services in small churches in the surrounding area, where I spent a few hectic minutes trying to determine in which key I could play each song so as to minimize the number of dead keys on the very old, poorly maintained pianos. The people in those churches are fair-minded, warm, and compassionate. I could fill a book with tales of their extraordinary kindness and generosity. Most of them are also very conservative; they oppose abortion, gay rights, government welfare programs, and most other liberal policies. Although I am no longer part of that culture, I respect, admire, and love the people there.

Yet I also came of age politically in the late 1960s and was shaped by the civil rights, antiwar, feminist, and environmental movements. I strongly oppose most of the policy agenda of the Christian Right. I want my daughter and son to grow up in a world in which they have equal access to a wider range of roles than society now provides. I want my gay and lesbian friends to live free of discrimination based on whom they love. I want the public schools to teach my children to think for themselves, to be tolerant of diverse lifestyles, and to know about the latest scientific thinking. Thus my political values are in conflict with my roots, and I engage in much internal debate when I write about the Christian Right.

I hope this internal dialogue has produced a fair assessment of the role of the Christian Right in American politics and the dilemmas it creates for the polity. If the book is balanced, I owe a great debt to John Green, who engaged in a protracted dialogue and sometimes debate through e-mail. John read and commented on the first draft of the book, served as a sounding board for my arguments, and kept me from saying some silly things from time to time. He ran data to help me test some questions I was asking.

A number of other people offered valuable comments. Ted Jelen, Matt Moen, and my wife, Elizabeth Cook, read the entire manuscript and made useful suggestions. Mary Bendyna also read early drafts of some chapters and helped me craft a better book. The series editor, Sandy Maisel, and the staff of Westview provided invaluable advice and assistance. The second edition of the book owes a great debt to Rachel Goldberg, who served as my research assistant for much of the time leading up to the book's completion.

I wrote the first edition of this book while teaching a small seminar on the Christian Right at Georgetown University in the fall of 1995. The thirteen students in that class were a lively group who inspired me to rethink many questions, assisted me in locating important information, and helped remind me why I enjoy teaching.

This book is dedicated to my grandmother, Zoe Wilcox, and her two sisters, Beulah Musgrove and Grace Ice. Although these women lived quite different lives, they shared a lifelong interest in learning and teaching. Their strength, compassion, decency, and love of life inspire me daily.

Clyde Wilcox

1

....

Introduction:
The Christian Right
in Context

Many signs point to the unraveling of a value system
that has served us so well since the Pilgrims landed at
Plymouth Rock in 1620. These developments . . . are
being orchestrated with great care by those who hate the
Christian system of values and are passionately
dedicated to its destruction. A formidable army has been
assembled . . . including the gay and lesbian movement;
the National Organization for Women and its minions;
the American Civil Liberties Union; People for the
American Way; the Mafia . . . the medical personnel who
are slaughtering our unborn babies; the euthanasia
organizations that are urging us to kill the old, the sick,
the handicapped. . . . These are the shock troops arrayed
in full battle gear before us.

—James C. Dobson,
fundraising letter for Focus on the Family, May 1988

George W. Bush seeks the support of the Christian Coalition early in his 2000 presidential campaign.

T HE 1995 CHRISTIAN COALITION ROAD TO VICTORY convention took place during a time of great optimism and confidence for the group's activists and leaders. Ralph Reed, then the group's executive director, told the cheering crowd that his goal was to make the **Christian Coalition** more powerful in the GOP than "the AFL-CIO or the radical feminists" in the Democratic party. (Broder, 1995). Pat Robertson, the organization's founder, set high goals: substantial influence in GOP party organizations in all fifty states and ten trained workers in every one of the 175,000 precincts in the United States (Edsall, 1995). A parade of presidential hopefuls addressed the 4,000 activists, and national party leaders praised the organization and its leaders for their role in American politics.

Four years later, at the 1999 Road to Victory convention Robertson told the gathered 3,500 activists that the Christian Coalition was making a comeback and that local chapters were growing very rapidly. Once again most GOP presidential candidates and GOP party leaders addressed the crowds. Yet no amount of enthusiastic applause could disguise the fact that the Christian Coalition was far weaker in 1999 than it had been in 1995.

In the interim the organization had lost its executive director, Reed, who left to form his own political consulting firm, and lost the two men who had taken his place. Other national staff had left as well, as had many state directors and an even greater number of county and local chapter leaders. Where once the Christian Coalition had active organizations in every state, the *New York Times* reported that the Coalition had strong affiliates in no more than seven states (Goodstein, 1999). After losing a long-running battle to gain tax-exempt status, the Coalition was beginning a reorganization that would divide the group into a section that could accept tax-exempt contributions and another section that would take taxable donations to finance the Coalition's voter guides.

The diminished stature of the Christian Coalition appeared to some observers to signal the end of the Christian Right, at least in the near term. Yet it is far too early to write the obituary, and there are several reasons to suspect that the Christian Right is not finished.

First, in many states movement activists have left the Christian Coalition but have joined other organizations such as affiliates of the Family Research Council.

The Coalition's difficulties have provided opportunities for competing groups. Second, public support for the movement has not been affected by the organizational difficulties of the Coalition, suggesting that the organization could indeed stage a comeback or a new organization could arise to take its place. Finally, the movement has deep roots in the GOP—both in the bureaucracy of the party and in its elected officials. The long list of presidential candidates who addressed the convention and who exhorted the activists was a clear testimony that most candidates believed that the Christian Right remains a critical electoral bloc in GOP politics.

In fact, media accounts of the influence of the Christian Right have gyrated wildly between underestimating the movement's considerable resources and overstating its numbers and impact. In 1995, most accounts supported the claims by Ralph Reed and others that the Christian Right had helped the Republicans gain control of the House of Representatives for the first time in a generation and to win back control of the U.S. Senate (Wilcox, 1995). Just three years earlier, in 1992, many commentators blamed Christian conservatives for damaging President George Bush's chances for reelection by using divisive and often extreme rhetoric at the Republican national convention.

In 1980, after Ronald Reagan won the White House with a margin that surprised pollsters, the media credited Jerry Falwell and the **Moral Majority** with the Republican victory. Journalists "discovered" the strengths of the Christian Right, and some painted the Moral Majority as a juggernaut that represented a substantial portion of the American citizenry. But public opinion polls soon revealed that Jerry Falwell was one of the most unpopular men in America, and journalists then "discovered" the weakness of the Christian Right. They painted the movement as small, extreme, and so deeply fragmented that further growth was impossible. By 1983 the media pronounced the Christian Right moribund. In 1984, when Jerry Falwell, Pat Robertson, and their followers were visible presences at the Republican nominating convention, the media rediscovered the assets of the Christian Right, only to rediscover its weaknesses by 1986. Early in the 1988 presidential campaign, when Pat Robertson did surprisingly well in the very early Michigan balloting and placed second in the Iowa caucuses, the media again discovered a hidden army of Christian Right activists. At the end of the campaign, when Robertson had spent more money than any other candidate but won only a handful of delegates, the weakness of the Christian Right was again the story. In late 1988, with a moderate Republican in the White House, Robertson back on television, and the Moral Majority essentially bankrupt, the media wrote the obituary of the movement. Journalists were not alone; some scholars also saw the movement as moribund at various points in its history and depicted its downfall as inevitable (Bruce, 1988).

In fact, public support for the Christian Right and its issue agenda has probably not changed a great deal since the formation of the Moral Majority in the late 1970s. What *has* changed is the sophistication of movement leaders and the presence of grassroots organizations. Between 10 percent and 15 percent of whites support the Christian Right and have done so since the formation of the Moral Majority in 1979 (Wilcox, 1992; Wilcox, DeBell, and Sigelman 1999). Yet the organizations of the Christian Right became more effective in enlisting some of those supporters into activism and in providing informational cues for voting.

The movement has important assets and weaknesses. It is likely that the fiery speeches by Christian Right leaders at the Republican national convention in 1992 hurt the GOP in that election and that the quiet mobilization of Christian conservatives in the 1994 elections helped the Republicans win a number of closely contested House and Senate races.[1] This disjunction occurred because highly visible efforts by the Christian Right prompt a countermobilization among liberals and moderates, whereas quiet efforts to mobilize **evangelicals** change the composition of the electorate without increasing participation by the movement's opponents.

What Is the Christian Right?

The Christian Right is a social movement that attempts to mobilize evangelical Protestants and other orthodox Christians into conservative political action. Many Christian Right leaders object to the term "Christian Right," which they believe depicts a narrow movement. Some prefer the term "religious Right," which would encompass all "people of faith" including conservative Jews and possibly Muslims. Yet despite the visible presence of orthodox Jews at Christian Coalition conventions, the movement remains concentrated primarily among white evangelical Christians (Green, 1995). Others object to both "Christian Right" and "religious Right" on the grounds that labeling the movement as part of the "Right" paints it as being outside the political mainstream. Ralph Reed prefers the term "Christian conservative," but many conservative Christians oppose the Christian Coalition and similar organizations. Other Christian Right leaders insist that theirs is truly a "pro-family" movement, although the agenda of the Christian Right includes many issues unrelated to the health of American families, and many liberals believe that Christian Right policies would harm families. I use the term "Christian Right" in this book without any necessary implication that the movement lies outside the American mainstream.

Like all social movements, the Christian Right is composed of social movement organizations, leaders, activists, and members, and it seeks to attract support from a broad potential constituency. Robert Zwier argued that "the primary audience, or constituency, for these groups was the approximately 50 million evangelicals in the country, and in particular the fundamentalist wing of that community. The aim from the beginning was to mobilize a group of people who had traditionally avoided politics because they saw it as dirty, corrupt business . . . by convincing people that political involvement was a God-given responsibility" (Zwier, 1984, pp. 9–10).

Movement leaders were and remain more ambitious, seeking an even larger constituency. Jerry Falwell spoke of appealing to "Catholics, Jews, Protestants, Mormons, and fundamentalists." Ralph Reed and the Christian Coalition made major efforts to expand its appeal to mainline Protestants, Catholics, African Americans, and Jews.

It is important to distinguish among movement leaders, movement activists, movement supporters, and the potential constituency of the Christian Right. Media accounts frequently equate the Christian Right with all born-again Christians. Such stories greatly exaggerate the movement's strength, for there are many born-again evangelical Christians in the United States. But some white evangelicals oppose the Christian Right, many are neutral to the movement, a sizable minority are supportive, and a much smaller number are active members. Evangelicals are best thought of as the core of the potential constituency of the Christian Right.

The organizations of the Christian Right are national groups, such as the Christian Coalition, the Family Research Council, and countless state and local organizations. The movement's leaders are people like Pat Robertson, James Dobson, Beverly LaHaye, head of Concerned Women for America, and Gary Bauer. Its activists are those who volunteer their time and money to work for these groups, and the members are those who have joined the organizations but are not active. The strength of the Christian Right lies in its activist base, which distributes voter guides in churches across America, and even those who have never considered joining the Christian Right may be influenced by the information in those voter guides.

Social movements are decentralized, differentiated, and sometimes disorganized. John Green, a political scientist , observed, "There are many modes of mobilization, many pools of resources, many sources of complaint, differential goals and beliefs, and a wide variety of activities, all occurring more or less simultaneously and more or less spontaneously."[2] Thus, no one organization or spokesperson represents the movement: Although the Christian Coalition has received the lion's share of media exposure, there are many Christian Right activists who are not members of the Coalition or supporters of Pat Robertson.

Moreover, the Christian Right has no single agenda but rather a collection of overlapping agendas. Some Christian Right activists focus almost entirely on ending abortions in America; others are concerned primarily with their efforts at homeschooling their children. Some are motivated to fight what they call the "radical homosexual agenda"; others seek to reduce the amount of sexual material in television, movies, and popular music. Some seek to promote a role for religion in public life: prayer in public schools, nativity scenes on city property, and a public acknowledgment that the United States is a Christian (or sometimes Judeo-Christian) nation.[3] Some activists care about all of these issues and more, whereas others focus on one issue to the exclusion of others.

As has been the case with other social movements, some elements of the Christian Right have institutionalized into more enduring structures. The Christian Coalition styles itself as an interest group, and former director Ralph Reed variously called the group the "Christian Chamber of Commerce" or the "Christian AFL-CIO." The organization has a clear structure and hierarchy, a national lobbying staff, and far more central control over the state and local units than did the earlier Moral Majority. The Christian Coalition often behaves like other interest groups, lobbying Democrats as well as Republicans and sometimes entering into unusual coalitions. In its effort to defeat lobby registration and campaign finance reform, for example, the Christian Coalition worked with the **American Civil Liberties Union**, although the latter is perhaps the most frequently cited "enemy" in the coalition's direct-mail fundraising.

Part of the institutionalization process is training leaders and even members in the norms of political action. Organizational leaders have sought to distance the group from activists who make extremist statements in public and to discipline the organization to behave well in political activity. When newly mobilized homeschool advocates threw ice at speakers at the Virginia Republican nominating convention in 1993, Ralph Reed quickly pointed out that the hecklers were not members of the Christian Coalition but rather backers of a homeschool advocate, Michael Farris (Rozell and Wilcox, 1996).

While part of the Christian Right is institutionalizing into interest groups, another part has become a major faction within Republican party politics. Although movement leaders sometimes insist for tax purposes that theirs is a nonpartisan movement, it is clear that the Christian Right is active almost exclusively within the GOP. This was not always true: The most visible spokesman for an earlier manifestation of the Christian Right in the 1920s was William Jennings Bryan, a perennial Democratic presidential candidate. When Pat Robertson first entered politics, he backed a candidate who sought to win the Democratic nomination. In addition, Robertson's father was a Democratic senator.

Yet at the turn of the twenty-first century the movement was so identified with the Republican party that Allen Hertzke described an incident when a Christian activist told a Christian Coalition gathering that his brother was a strong Christian and a Democratic officeholder, only to be greeted by stunned silence (Hertzke, 1993). Christian Right activists flocked to the Republican party in 1980 as the Moral Majority mobilized for Ronald Reagan, and they participated in greater numbers in 1988 as Robertson sought the GOP presidential nomination. Some of these early activists retired from politics over the next decade, but others remained active in the party.

Going into the 2000 election, Christian conservatives constituted an identifiable **party faction** in the national and most state Republican parties. In states such as Virginia and Minnesota, the party remained deeply divided between a moderate group and a Christian conservative faction, with considerable animosity on both sides. In other states, such as Washington, the anger subsided but the division endured. In still other states such as South Carolina, the Christian Right was well integrated into the party, and many moderates appeared to have made peace with the movement's influence.[4] In some states, the Christian Right served as part of a larger coalition of conservative groups that opposed the more moderate elements of the party. In other states, the Christian Right constituted one of two opposing factions, with all other elements of the party arrayed against them.

As a party faction, the Christian Right contends with moderates for control of nominations; control in turn leads to access to campaign resources and party platforms. The Christian Right provides the Republicans with a pool of potential voters and volunteers and a ready communications network and infrastructure. But these resources come with a price, for in most elections in which Christian Right activists have won their party's nomination, they have lost the general election.

The Context

Is the Christian Right good or bad for America? This question inspires answers from Christian conservatives and their opponents that differ radically in substance but are similar in passion. Among those familiar with the Christian Right, the movement is the source of great controversy.

The Christian Right attracts controversy for several reasons. First, its central social agenda includes issues that are among the most heated in American politics. Christian Right activists generally seek to sharply limit and eventually ban access to legal abortions, to eliminate all laws that protect gays and lesbians from job and housing discrimination, and to alter the curriculum in the public schools in a variety of areas ranging from sex education to history and sociology to biology and geology. The agenda of most Christian Right groups includes many other issues as well, but abortion, gay rights, and education fuel the greatest enthusiasm. These are issues about which many Americans care passionately and upon which the public is deeply divided. On each issue there are well-organized, well-funded interest groups that represent many Americans who oppose the Christian Right agenda.

Second, some citizens object to the general effort to mobilize conservative Christians into political action. They do so for varied reasons. Some believe that America is a secular society and that religious values should not play a role in the public debate. For others, religious values have a place in politics, but religious leaders should not become political leaders, and churches should not be the locus of political mobilization. Still others believe that religious values and leaders should play an active role in politics but are offended by claims by the Christian Coalition and others to speak for all Christians.[5] They argue that the Bible does not contain passages calling for a flat tax or opposing government health care for the poor, positions advocated by Christian Right organizations.

Although the Christian Coalition takes conservative positions on these economic issues, many other Christians take the opposite positions and derive their views from their religious beliefs. Catholics may follow the teachings of the church on the need to care for the poor, and liberal Protestants may point to biblical passages that uphold the virtues of the poor while criticizing the values of the rich. These Christians may object to having an organization called the Christian Coalition presume to speak for them in politics and to take positions that some Christian Right activists believe are the "true Christian" stands.

Finally, the Christian Right is controversial because of the heated rhetoric that its leaders and especially its most ardent activists sometimes produce. Robertson, for example, strikes fear in the hearts of moderate Republicans when he promises to take over all fifty state party committees or when he writes that "a small, well-organized minority can influence the selection of candidates to an astonishing degree."[6] Ralph Reed, in explaining the success of the "stealth" candidates who won election to San Diego's school boards, claimed that "I do guerrilla warfare. I paint my face and travel at night. You don't know it's over until election night" (Blumenthal, 1994, p. 114). [7]

On a variety of issues, Christian Right activists have taken quite extreme positions, and many Americans find their rhetoric to be threatening. Feminist mothers and wives recoiled when newspapers published a quotation from one of Pat Robertson's fundraising letters in which he claimed "the feminist agenda is not

about equal rights for women. It is about a socialist, anti-family political movement that encourages women to leave their husbands, kill their children, practice
witchcraft, destroy capitalism, and become lesbians."[8] Robertson's rhetoric about
gays and lesbians has been similarly vitriolic, and some local and state leaders
have advocated very harsh treatment of homosexuals.

Christian Right activists argue, quite correctly, that *all* organizations that raise
money through direct mail seek to demonize their political opponents, because
such appeals result in more effective fundraising. Indeed, liberal groups such as
People for the American Way and the ACLU make fundraising appeals that cari-
cature Christian conservatives and seek to heighten fear of the Christian Right.
Christian Right rhetorical appeals may be no more extreme than those of their
political opponents, but they nevertheless make many citizens uneasy.

Of course, controversy is not necessarily a bad thing. If debate over the Christian Right stimulates Americans to deal with their core values and inspires the
nation to consider its policies in light of those values, then something worthwhile
would be achieved. But critics charge that the Christian Right stirs up intolerance,
sexism, and homophobia and that its involvement in politics is therefore a net
detriment to the public discourse.

In the introduction to his thoughtful and balanced book about a legal struggle
between Christian conservatives and educators over textbooks in the Hawkins
County, Tennessee, schools, Stephen Bates posed one variant of the dilemma of
the Christian Right. "How should a secular, tolerant state cope with devout but
intolerant citizens, both in the public schools and in the public square" (Bates,
1993, p. 12)? The answer to this question depends critically on how we character-
ize the Christian Right—as a defensive movement seeking to protect the religious
liberties of conservative Christians or as an offensive movement seeking to impose a narrow morality on all Americans.

Although Christian Right leaders use different rhetorical appeals to different
groups, they frequently argue that theirs is a *defensive* movement—one designed
to protect their moral values and especially their ability to impart those values to
their children. Many see their beliefs and values ridiculed in mainstream media,
undermined in schools, and ignored by a consumer culture that promotes a mul-
ticulturalism that appears to have no room for evangelical culture.

For its supporters, the Christian Right is an attempt to restore Judeo-Christian
values to a country that is in deep moral decline. They quote William Bennett,
former secretary of education in the Reagan administration: "We are in a race
between civilization and catastrophe. . . . We have record murder and violent
crime rates, huge increases in births to unwed mothers, educational decline, bro-
ken families. . . . All of this, and we are told that the very religious are those we

must fear. Religion is on the side of civilization; more people ought to begin to realize it."[9] Christian Right supporters believe that society suffers from the lack of a firm basis of Judeo-Christian values and seek to write laws that embody those values.

Ralph Reed maintains that "people of faith are not. . . asking people to subscribe to their theology; they are asking them to subscribe to their public policy views, and to respect their right to participate without their religion being impugned" (Reed, 1994a, p. 41). He argued that the Christian Coalition merely seeks to have "a seat at the table," not to dominate discussion around that table. He characterizes the agenda of the Christian Right as a mainstream agenda and argues that Christian conservatives want what most Americans want—stronger families, safety from crime, successful schools, and democracy.

The Christian Coalition describes its purposes as follows:

1. To represent Christians before local councils, state legislatures, and the U.S. Congress.
2. To train Christians for effective political action.
3. To inform Christians of timely issues and legislation.
4. To speak out in the public arena and the media.
5. To protest anti-Christian bigotry.[10]

Its work in mobilizing conservative Christians to vote, the Coalition claims, "is no different from the League of Women Voters, the National Organization for Women, NARAL, the AFL-CIO, or Jesse Jackson's Rainbow Coalition."[11]

Although many movement activists describe a defensive movement seeking to protect religious liberties, other Christian Right activists concede that they seek to apply their moral views to all Americans. Gary Bauer, head of the Family Research Council and presidential candidate in 1999, noted

"So the question is not whether you legislate morality. The question is whose morality you're going to legislate. Somebody's values are going to win. We just have to have the confidence to get in the public square and say that our values will be best for the country." (*New York Times*, August 17, 1999, A12)

Critics of the movement take a different view and charge that the Christian Right is an intolerant movement seeking to impose a narrow, sectarian morality on America. Some describe the Christian Right as a reactionary movement that would censor books, throw gays and lesbians into jail, and confine women to the kitchen.[12] Soon after the 1994 elections, the Reverend Jesse Jackson charged that conservative white Christians who used the Bible to justify slavery were "the

Christian Coalition of the time" and that "the Christian Coalition was a strong force in Germany . . . . it laid down a suitable scientific, theological rationale for the tragedy in Germany."[13]

If the Christian Right is a defensive movement that seeks to protect religious liberties of conservative Christians, then there can be no question it has an obvious place at the bargaining table of American politics. If, on the other hand, the movement seeks to deprive gays and lesbians of their civil rights, to limit dramatically the public and private role of women in society, and to impose a prescientific worldview on public education, then some would argue that its policy demands are illegitimate and outside the mainstream of American politics and should therefore not be part of serious policy discussion.

Ultimately, many Americans fear the Christian Right because they see some movement activists issuing harsh condemnations of Americans whose lifestyles differ from those that conservative Christians espouse. They see local organizations working to remove books from public libraries and to prohibit the teaching of *The Wizard of Oz* in public schools because it contains a character who is a "good witch." They hear some of the more extreme movement activists suggesting that known homosexuals be imprisoned, and they watch television accounts of the assassination of abortion providers by those on the fringe of the pro-life movement. To at least some observers, these extremists do indeed echo Nazi persecution of gays and public book burnings.

In the 1980s, Margaret Atwood in *The Handmaid's Tale* wrote of a future in which the Christian Right had triumphed and women were subservient to men. Doctors who provided abortions were executed, and women were taught that rape victims deserved their fate because they had enticed men. Atwood's nightmare world is a far cry from Reed's description of the Christian Right agenda. This disjuncture between the soothing reassurances of Reed and the overheated fears of the Left has made the Christian Right one of the most controversial actors in American politics.

Debates between religious conservatives and other citizens occur in many countries and regions of the world. Catholic conservatives debate moderates and liberals about abortion policy in Ireland and Italy, Islamic fundamentalists debate modernists in Iran and Saudi Arabia, orthodox Jews debate secular Jews in Israel, and Sikh fundamentalists debate Hindu fundamentalists and Muslims in India. Yet to understand the debate about the role of the American Christian Right, it is helpful to consider the American context. This includes America's unique policies on church and state, the religious diversity of the United States, and its tradition of civil religion.

The First Amendment and Church and State

The debate about the role of the Christian Right in America is located in a larger debate about the role of religion in American politics. The debate is an ongoing one—indeed, it took place in the American colonies before the drafting of the Constitution and the Bill of Rights and has been reengaged at various points throughout U.S. history. At stake are two competing visions for American democracy: One holds that the United States is a Christian nation specially blessed by God; the other maintains that it is a secular state with a high wall of separation between church and state.

The First Amendment to the U.S. Constitution states in part: "Congress shall make no law respecting an establishment of religion, or prohibiting the free exercise thereof." The first phrase is generally referred to as the **establishment clause** and the second as the **free exercise clause**. These sixteen words, written over 200 years ago, have inspired millions of words in a sometimes heated debate over what these two clauses should mean. Scholars have emphasized the precise wording of the amendment—sometimes focusing on a single word, such as *an* establishment of religion or *respecting* an establishment of religion, or highlighting the contrast between *prohibiting* the free exercise of religion and the stricter *abridging* freedom of speech (Malbin, 1978; Levy, 1986). They have debated the original intent of the founders and whether those intentions should bind a country that is far more religiously pluralistic than it was two centuries earlier.

In general, we can distinguish between two positions on each of the two clauses. Those who debate the meaning of the establishment clause generally hold accommodationist or separationist positions. **Accommodationists** believe that the Constitution merely prohibits the establishment of a national religion. They point out that many colonies had established churches at the time of the founding and indeed for many years afterward. They argue that the First Amendment merely prohibits the government from tilting to one religious group over another but does not mean that the government may not prefer religion generally to non-religion.

Although accommodationists claim the government must merely be neutral among religions, the specifics of their arguments usually imply that the government need remain neutral only among religions in the Judeo-Christian tradition and sometimes only among Christian faiths.[14] They quote with approval Alexis de Tocqueville, who wrote in 1835, "Christian morality is everywhere the same . . . . Christianity, therefore, reigns without obstacle, by universal consent; the consequence is. . . that every principle of the moral world is fixed and determinate, although the political world is abandoned to the debates and experiments of men" (Tocqueville, 1945, pp. 314–315). Thus the Judeo-Christian tradition is seen as giving moral coherence to the nation.

Separationists, in contrast, emphasize the potential of religion to lead to violent conflict. They note that James Madison, an early Federalist leader and later president whose essays on the Constitution are still studied by political scientists and constitutional scholars, listed religion as a potential source of divisive factions in *Federalist No. 10.* In addition, separationists argue that the First Amendment prescribes what Thomas Jefferson later called a "high wall of separation" between church and state. They quote with approval Justice Hugo Black's opinion in *Everson v. Board of Education* (1947): "Neither a state nor the federal government can set up a church. Neither can pass laws which aid one religion, aid all religions, or prefer one religion over another."

Although conservatives frequently portray separationists as hostile to religion, Jefferson believed that religion would benefit from separation. He argued that "true" religion would thrive in direct competition with other religious creeds, whereas "false" religion needed protection by the state (Wills, 1990). Others have argued that religion can better play its prophetic role as critic of the state when there is little entanglement between the two (Jelen, 1991a).

Accommodationists and separationists differ in their views of the proper public role for religion. Most accommodationists think that prayers are acceptable in public schools at graduation ceremonies and sporting events. They favor public displays of nativity scenes at Christmas and other open public support for religion. They argue that as long as these prayers are nonsectarian and a Jewish candelabrum called a **menorah** is displayed along with the nativity scene, the government has not endorsed any particular religion. Few would go so far as to allow Hindu or Buddhist prayers in public schools, however, and this stance suggests there are limits to just how neutral they believe government should be (Jelen and Wilcox, 1995). Separationists would oppose all of these public displays of religion, arguing that any endorsement of religion by government is a violation of constitutional guarantees.

There are also two basic positions on the free exercise clause: One would allow all kinds of religious activity so long as no one is harmed; the other would limit such activities to those within some broadly defined community consensus. **Libertarians** hold that all kinds of religious practices are protected, including those of non-Christian groups. They would support the right of Sikh schoolchildren to wear special religious headgear to school, of Muslim girls to cover their heads in gym class, of Santerians to sacrifice animals to their gods. **Communitari-**

ans would argue that religious freedom for minority religious groups should be limited by community norms. If state law prohibits the use of peyote in an effort to control drug use, then Native Americans should not use it in their age-old ceremonies, and if the U.S. Army denies recruits the right to any special attire, then orthodox Jews should not wear special religious headgear.

Of course, many issues fall between these two clauses, evoking both establishment and free exercise claims. For example, when student religious groups ask to use school property to hold their meetings after school, is this a question of establishment (using taxpayer funds to keep the building open) or of free exercise (allowing students to practice their religion)? Over the past several years, Christian Right groups have increasingly framed their concerns around free exercise issues rather than establishment ones. For example, instead of arguing that all schoolchildren would benefit from a public prayer to begin their school day (an establishment issue), Christian conservatives now argue that their children are being prevented from offering up audible prayers (a free exercise issue).

Most Christian Right activists take accommodationist positions on the establishment clause and communitarian stands on the free exercise clause, making them what some scholars have called **Christian preferentialists** (Jelen and Wilcox, 1995). These individuals want a public role for Christian symbols and practices but resist the notion of non-Christian groups having equal access to public support.

Christian Right leaders, however, frequently endorse a position of **religious nonpreferentialism,** which holds that all religious groups have a place in the public square. Ralph Reed wrote: "America is not solely a Christian nation, but a pluralistic society of Protestants, Catholics, Jews, Muslims, and other people of faith whose broader culture once honored religion, but which today increasingly reflects a hostility toward faith in the public square" (Reed, 1994a, p. 135).

It is important to understand that those who oppose the Christian Right are not universally opposed to religion or even to a role for religion in public life. But many do oppose the Christian Right because they believe the policies it promotes violate the separation between church and state and might infringe on the free exercise rights of religious minorities.

The debate over the role of the Christian Right in America is often framed within this broader debate on the role of religion in American public life. Those who support the Christian Right see contemporary society as aggressively secular and generally hostile to religious values and expression. Those who oppose the Christian Right believe that the movement seeks an unconstitutional establishment of one set of religious views.

Religion and Politics in America

America is unique among Western democracies in the intensity of its moral politics. Compared with other industrialized democracies, America is remarkable for both its religious diversity and the strength of its religious institutions. Many European countries have established churches, and in those countries the majority of believers are members. Large majorities of citizens in the nations of southern Europe are Catholic, and large majorities of those in Scandinavia are Lutheran. Germany is nearly evenly divided between Lutherans in the north and Catholics in the south. In no country are there more than three or four dominant religious groups.

In contrast, Americans belong to an almost bewildering array of churches. Many states and regions have clear religious majorities—Baptists in the South, Catholics in New England, Mormons in Utah—but every state has churches representing dozens of Protestant denominations. Moreover, in urban areas on the East and West Coasts, there are growing numbers of Muslims, Hindus, Sikhs, Buddhists, and others from outside the Judeo-Christian tradition.

Not only is America a religiously diverse country, but it is also one in which religious belief and practice are unusually common. International surveys show that more than half of Americans indicate that God is extremely important to their life, compared with fewer than 20 percent of citizens in France, Britain, Italy, Spain, and Sweden (Wilcox, 1988b). Americans attend church more often than citizens in most other industrialized democracies, pray more often, and read their Bibles more frequently.

Some have argued that it is precisely the religious diversity of America that sustains its rich religious life. In nations where one church enjoys monopoly status, that church may grow "lazy" and make little effort to seek new converts. In the United States, in contrast, Baptist, Methodist, Presbyterian, and Assembly of God pastors may compete in a small community for the same potential flock of congregants and therefore try much harder to attract and keep new members (Finke and Stark, 1992).

The combination of this religious diversity and intensity creates an atmosphere in which moral issues are hotly contested because there are competing moral visions, each with devoted adherents. Yet underlying the diversity of American religion is a more general support for its basic civil religion.

America remains a nation with a strongly established **civil religion**. Religious imagery, language, and concepts pervade public discourse, appear on currency, and are present in the pledge to the flag. Many Christians see America as somehow chosen by God to fulfill His will. The Puritans frequently likened their new covenant with God to that of God with Abraham and sought to create "God's New Israel." This infusion of religious belief and national purpose persists today.

Researchers have found that many children and adults alike agree with statements such as "America is God's chosen people today," "I consider holidays like the Fourth of July religious as well as patriotic," and "We should respect the president's authority since his authority is from God" (Wimberly, 1976; Smidt, 1980). In many Christian churches, American flags hang behind the pulpit, beside the Christian flag, and children in Sunday school classes pledge allegiance to both.

Those who support this civil religion generally believe that the president has a moral, prophetic role as well as a political one. Perhaps for this reason, surveys have shown that Americans would vote for candidates from many different religious backgrounds, but only a minority would vote for a candidate with no religious affiliation.[15] President Reagan often used religious language in his speeches, although he seldom attended church, and President Clinton called for a return to religious values in the public debate. Such public proclamations of the religious character of the nation are very much in keeping with its civil religion, and many Christian Right activists believe that the president has a unique role to play as moral as well as political leader of the nation. This view helps explain the vehemence with which Christian Right activists pressured Congress to impeach and remove President Clinton from office after it became clear that he had engaged in extra-marital sexual contact with a White House intern, and then lied about it on national television.

These tenets of civil religion are held by nearly all Christian Right activists and leaders and by many opponents of the movement as well. Civil religion provides an undercurrent of unity beneath the choppy waters of religious diversity. Yet the precise meaning of this civil religion is contested in America, with moderates focusing on the melting pot of religious diversity and the Christian Right centering instead on the idea that Americans are God's chosen people.

The belief that there is a religious character to the American polity has important consequences for Christian conservatives. If America is God's new chosen nation, then Christian Right leaders may be likened to the prophets of the Old Testament, who repeatedly called on Israel to repent. When their warnings were ignored, God inflicted various punishments described in the Old Testament.

Jerry Falwell has sounded this theme:

> The rise and fall of nations confirm to the Scripture. . . . Psalm 9:17 admonishes "The wicked shall be turned into hell, and all the nations that forget God." America will be no exception. If she forgets God, she too will face His wrath and judgement like every other nation in the history of humanity. But we have the promise of Psalm 33:12, which declares "Blessed is the nation whose name is the Lord." When a nation's ways

please the Lord, that nation is blessed with supernatural help (Falwell, 1981, pp. 24–25).

Many activists see their role as that of "redeeming America" (Lienesch, 1994), calling it to repent for many sins and directing it to the path of salvation. Thus, Christian conservatives interpret elements of America's civil religion as mandating their political activity.

Although most Americans expect their political leaders to express religious sentiments, the public is more deeply divided about whether preachers and churches should be involved in politics. Nearly one in four Americans would not vote for a minister even if the person were from their party and shared their political views, and a somewhat larger number oppose the involvement of preachers in a variety of specific political activities. Liberals and conservatives alike are more likely to disapprove of political action by religious leaders if they disagree with the substance of the policies: one survey revealed that conservative evangelicals are very supportive of ministers being active in pro-life or antipornography demonstrations but far less likely to approve of involvement to end apartheid in South Africa, whereas liberals are more supportive of antiapartheid activity and less so of pro-life activism (Jelen and Wilcox, 1995).

Both liberal and conservative Christians have been quite critical of the political involvement of churches on the other side of the aisle. Conservative clerics decried the involvement of liberal churches in the civil rights and antiwar movements of the 1960s and argued that preachers should never be involved in politics. When those same preachers became involved with the Christian Right in the 1980s, it was the liberal pastors who denounced such action as violating the primary mission of the church. In fact, American churches have long been involved in crusades of moral reform, including fights over slavery, racial segregation, abortion, and Prohibition.

However, some churches defended slavery, alcohol, segregation, and abortion rights, and it is this division among religious institutions that troubles many religious professionals. For every position of the Christian Right, there is a Christian religious body in America that takes a very different view. For this reason, many liberals resent the term "Christian" Coalition, for they believe that the Christian Right movement claims to speak for all Christians but in fact represents the views of only one segment of the Christian community.

The debate over the role of the Christian Right takes place within the context of this uniquely American religious pluralism and civil religion. Christian Right activists proclaim their worldview loudly because it competes with so many different worldviews, many derived from different religious traditions. The activists seek to redeem an America that they view as the new chosen land. Opponents point to the many diverse religious views in America and argue that it is best for the state to leave many moral questions to individual choice and to remain neutral as the many diverse traditions compete for adherents.

A Culture War?

Many Christian Right activists and some social scientists see America engaged in a culture war between highly religious citizens and secular citizens. More than a quarter of Americans say they attend church at least weekly, and a third report that religion influences their daily lives "a great deal." These numbers are far higher than in most other Western democracies and validate claims that America is a highly religious nation. Yet many other Americans have no attachment to religious institutions, never attend church except for weddings and other ceremonies, and report that religion is not important in their lives. Others have only marginal involvement in religion. More than four in ten Americans report that religion provides at best "some" guidance in their lives and that they attend church rarely. This relatively secular set of Americans is seen as in conflict with those with deep religious convictions.[16]

A noted sociologist, James Davison Hunter, described these two groups as being engaged in a culture war that affects public policy and individual lives (Hunter, 1991). He argued that the conflict is rooted in different worldviews—in different beliefs about moral authority between orthodox and progressive Americans. Although Hunter included many deeply religious Americans in his progressive category, many Christian Right leaders and some scholars have recast his argument as a battle between religious and nonreligious Americans.

Yet the idea of a culture war oversimplifies the dimensions of conflict over social and moral issues. It is clear that secular and highly religious Americans do differ in their views on political issues such as abortion, gay rights, and school prayer, but it is also true that many deeply religious Americans differ on these issues as well. Not all deeply religious Catholics agree on church doctrine, for example. Among Catholics who attend church services every week, there is a sizable pro-choice contingent, and an even larger group favors passage of laws to bar job discrimination against gays and lesbians, even though abortion and homosexuality are disapproved by church teaching.[17]

Moreover, it is not the case that secular Americans are uniformly hostile to religion. One study of attitudes on church-state issues reported that most secular citizens were generally supportive of the rights of religious expression and were actually more supportive of the rights of fundamentalist preachers to speak on college campuses than were white evangelicals (Jelen and Wilcox, 1995). Although there clearly is cultural conflict in America, there are many sides to that conflict, and the Christian Right represents only one of them.

In addition, many Americans are what some have called "noncombatants" in the culture war. A sizable number of Americans would like to restore religious values to public life but resist efforts by Christian Right groups to dictate the nature and meaning of those values. They are not moved by claims of the Left that the Christian Right is a "radical, extreme" movement that constitutes a clear and present danger to America, but they are also unconvinced that American culture discriminates against Christians and that "radical liberals" are seeking to take away religious freedom.

Conclusion and Overview of the Book

These broader contexts help us understand the nuances of the dilemma of the Christian Right. Movement proponents see the Christian Right as a defensive movement that seeks to represent the interests of evangelicals and other orthodox Christians in American politics. Acknowledging the religious diversity of America, Ralph Reed, former executive director of the Christian Coalition, claims a broader consensus on values among "people of faith" and suggests that secular Americans are waging a culture war on religious conservatives. He calls upon conservative Christians and others to help restore America's greatness by reestablishing the core values upon which the country was founded. Reed argues that the Christian Right merely seeks a seat at the table at which policy is negotiated, for the interests of conservative Christians are no different in kind from those of African Americans, feminists, business, or labor.

Critics of the movement argue that the Christian Right seeks to deny America's pluralism by establishing or restoring an orthodox Christian cultural hegemony. To these critics, the Christian Coalition represents one narrow segment of Christianity in a nation that also includes Jews, Muslims, Hindus, Buddhists, Sikhs, and secular citizens. They argue that the Christian Right seeks not to bargain at the table but to impose its narrow morality on all Americans. They charge that the Christian Right would establish a sectarian religion in America and that its adherents are the aggressors in any culture war because they seek to deny reproductive rights to women, civil rights protection to gays and lesbians, and opportunities to women.

In this chapter we have defined the Christian Right and discussed different ways to conceive of the movement. We have also defined the basic conflict over the role of the Christian Right in American politics and described the context in which the debate over that role takes place.

The contemporary Christian Right is in fact the fourth wave of conservative Christian activity during the twentieth century. In the next chapter we place the Christian Right in historical context, compare and contrast the movement with its earlier incarnations, and discuss the target constituency of the Christian Right.

Chapter 3 introduces the organizations of the Christian Right and their leaders. It also examines the activities of Christian Right groups, both in elections and in influencing government policy. I conclude with an assessment of the impact of the movement on public policy in America.

The dilemma of the Christian Right is explored in greater detail in chapter 4. I examine claims that the Christian Right has helped American democracy by bringing into political action a previously apolitical group of citizens and claims that Christian Right adherents do not share the democratic norms that are the basis for American politics. In addition, the chapter examines the issue agenda of the Christian Right and analyzes the ramifications if movement leaders achieved power.

In the final chapter I consider the future of the Christian Right and its issue agenda.

2

....

Revivals and Revolution: The Christian Right in Twentieth-Century America

If evolution wins, Christianity goes—not suddenly, of course, but gradually, for the two cannot stand together.

—William Jennings Bryan

T HE CHRISTIAN COALITION, FOCUS ON THE FAMILY, and Concerned Women for America are only the most recent of many conservative political organizations that have been formed out of the religious enthusiasms of white evangelical Protestantism. Throughout the twentieth century, the energy and influence of the Christian Right have ebbed and flowed. Many organizations claiming to represent the political views of white evangelicals have come and gone, and the latest incarnation of the Christian Right has some important similarities and differences compared with these earlier movements. To understand fully the Christian Right today, it is important to know more about the earlier movements.

The principal constituency for the Christian Right in the twentieth century has been white evangelical Christians, but within this broad category are many different theological groups, whose members not always gotten along with one another or supported the same political causes.. It is therefore useful to discuss the history of the religious movements that have created these divisions among white evangelicals and whose enthusiasms have frequently led to the formation of Christian Right groups.

The Fundamentalist Religious Revolt

Early in the twentieth century, two religious movements—fundamentalism and pentecostalism—emerged that would later provide the major constituencies for the Christian Right. The pentecostals did not become involved in politics until later in the century, but the **fundamentalist** movement quickly emerged as the vanguard of resistance to theological modernists. At the heart of the debate between fundamentalists and modernists was the way the church should respond to new scientific theories and discoveries, especially Darwin's articulation of the theory of evolution.

During the last decades of the nineteenth century, many of the clergy in the largest Protestant denominations began to embrace modern scientific and social ideas. Leading intellectuals in Protestant seminaries sought to make interpretation of Scripture consonant with the new understandings of science. These modernists also emphasized the web of social obligations that the church could fulfill. When some social thinkers transformed Darwin's descriptive theory of natural selection into a prescriptive theory that government should leave those who were less "fit" to their natural fate, many Protestant churches instead preached a **social gospel** of responsibility to the poor and disadvantaged. In this view, Darwin's theory implied that humans were perfectible, and the best way to pursue that perfection was to ameliorate the conditions of poverty and ignorance that helped create imperfection.

This emphasis on the social gospel was controversial, for religious conservatives resisted both the policy implications of these teachings and the shift of focus away from saving souls. The conservatives, who were initially a loose coalition of pietistic revivalists, conservative Calvinists, and other evangelicals, joined forces to publish *The Fundamentals* in 1910, a collection of essays in defense of orthodoxy. Although this collection went unnoticed in the media and among academics, it provided the intellectual underpinnings (and the name) of a new religious movement called fundamentalism. Over the next decade, the split between the conservatives and liberals widened, and in 1919 the conservatives formed the **World's Christian Fundamentals Association** (WCFA). This marked the beginning of a bitter religious battle between the fundamentalists and modernists.

The fundamentalist leadership, including William Riley, Clarence Dixon, and John Straton, instituted a series of more than one hundred conferences in the United States and Canada to preach the fundamentals. The Baptist and Presbyterian churches were deeply divided, and eventually each of these denominations split. The fundamentalists emphasized the need to remain pure and separate from the world—even separate from other nonfundamentalist Protestants.

At the core of fundamentalist doctrine were three ideas (Sandeen, 1970; Marsden, 1980; Jorstad, 1970). First, fundamentalists embraced **premillennialism**, a doctrine about the timing of the second coming of Christ. Premillennialists believed that the world must first worsen, and then an Antichrist would arise who would win power. Eventually, however, Christ would return and summon the faithful in the Rapture. At that time all true Christians, living or dead, would go immediately to heaven, leaving the "unsaved" to endure an unsavory time of tribulation on earth under the rule of the Antichrist. Soon Christ would return to lead the faithful in a successful battle with the Antichrist. Premillenialist eschatology is dramatized in a series of novels by Timothy LaHaye and Jerry Jenkins—*Left Behind* and its sequels, which have appeared on the *New York Times* bestseller lists.

In contrast, the doctrine of **postmillennialism** held that Christ would come again after the millennium, a thousand-year period of perfect peace. The debate between the premillennialists and postmillennialists had been heated in theologi-

cal circles for some time, but fundamentalist leaders staked a clear position on behalf of the premillennialists.

This seemingly technical doctrinal difference has important political consequences. If Christians must establish the millennium on earth before Christ
comes again, then politics becomes an essential Christian duty. Only by improv-
ing the state of the world can prophecy be fulfilled and the kingdom of heaven be
brought into existence. Christians should work for peace and justice in this world
in order to hasten the transition into the kingdom.

If, on the other hand, the world must inevitably worsen until Christ rescues his
followers, then politics is a futile endeavor. Moreover, if Christ might come again
at any moment and summon the pure to him, then the top priority for Christians
must be to remain distinct from the sinful world to avoid temptation.[1] Political
involvement might lead to compromise with sin, which would leave the Christian
unready for the trumpet call that would signal the second coming. The fundamentalist acceptance of premillennialism therefore created a strong resistance to
political involvement that the movement leaders have worked hard at various
times to overcome.

The second component of fundamentalist doctrine was **dispensationalism,** the
belief that God has dealt with humans under different covenants in different eras.
Most fundamentalists believed there were to be seven dispensations, and the
world was in its sixth. Because the seventh was the kingdom of heaven, dispensationalism served to heighten expectations that the Rapture, or second coming of
Christ, would occur very soon. Dispensationalism is an important source of fundamentalist disputes with pentecostals (discussed later in this section) and
thereby undermined the potential unity of the Christian Right in the 1980s
(Wills, 1990).

Third, fundamentalists believed that the way to know God's will was to study
the Bible, which was the inerrant word of God. Most accepted an even stronger
position—that every word of the Bible was literally true. The most politically
charged issue at the turn of the century that arose out of the literal interpretation
of the Bible was **creationism**—the teaching that the biblical creation story in Genesis is literally true. In the biblical account, the world was created in six days, and
Adam was made directly by God out of the dust of the ground, with Eve constructed from one of Adam's ribs. Many fundamentalists believed that the earth
was created on October 25, 4004 B.C., a date established in 1654 by Bishop Usher.

Although the literal interpretation of Genesis was once widely accepted among
American elites, in the late nineteenth and early twentieth centuries, scientific
theories that contradicted this reading gained prominence. Darwin's theory of
evolution gained acceptance among biologists; geologists began to read the earth's

history in strata of rocks, and most came to believe that the earth was far older than fundamentalist doctrine would suggest; and astrophysicists read the history of the universe from the light of distant stars and argued that the universe was billions of years old.

The heads of seminaries in the modernist denominations attempted to make peace with Darwin by arguing that although God had surely made the world, he did it over billions of years, not six days. They argued that the biblical account was a metaphor, not meant to be taken literally. Fundamentalists rejected the scientific theories, accepting by faith that the heavens and earth were created in six twenty-four-hour days. If the biblical account must be true, then scientific discoveries must be made consonant with biblical truth. In response to scientific evidence that the rocks of the earth were older than 6,000 years, for example, some fundamentalists countered that when God created the earth he preaged the rocks, or that the great flood of Noah disrupted the underlying geology of the earth (Brin, 1994; Numbers, 1992).

The fundamentalist movement generated enormous religious energy. Pietistic clergy preached the fundamentals in tent revivals throughout the South and Midwest, and individual congregations sometimes split apart as had their parent denomination. Some of these new churches affiliated with newly formed fundamentalist denominations; others remained as independent fundamentalist churches.

From these doctrinal elements and religious schisms, fundamentalists fashioned their most distinctive characteristic—a fervent **separatism**. Fundamentalists emphasized the importance of keeping themselves apart from the impure world and from doctrinally impure Christians as well. They stressed the importance of avoiding extensive contact with "unsaved" Americans, kept to their own churches and social networks, and began to fashion their own communication channels through publications, seminaries, and other means.

Although the fundamentalist movement attracted the most attention, the turn of the century was also the occasion for the birth of **pentecostalism**. As in the case of fundamentalism, pentecostal denominations were created out of schisms within Protestant churches.

Whereas the fundamentalists stressed the literal truth of Scripture, the pentecostals focused on the imminent power of God and especially of the Holy Spirit in their lives. The movement took its name from the biblical account of the day of Pentecost, the day the Holy Spirit was poured onto the disciples, who then spoke in tongues that people from all nations could understand.[2] In pentecostal belief the Holy Spirit imparts to many an additional blessing of special religious gifts.[3]

The most common of these gifts is **glossolalia,** or the speaking in tongues; others include faith healing, prophecy, and being "slain in the Spirit."[4]

The pentecostals shared with the fundamentalists an opposition to modernism and a belief in the inerrancy of Scriptures, and many pentecostals at the turn of the twentieth century considered themselves in some ways to be fundamentalists. Indeed, a variety of religious movements at the time endorsed the doctrinal orthodoxy of *The Fundamentals* and shared the fundamentalists' strong rejection of modernism.

But fundamentalist clergy violently rejected the pentecostal movement. At the core of the doctrinal dispute was dispensationalism—or rather a dispute about precisely which dispensation was in effect at the time. Many pentecostals believed that the "age of the Spirit" began in the early 1900s and marked a time when Christians should expect to receive spiritual gifts. In contrast, the fundamentalists believed that these gifts were part of an earlier dispensation at the time of the apostles and that speaking in tongues and faith healing were no longer legitimate spiritual practices.[5]

Although fundamentalists and pentecostals shared a large core of doctrine, the differences between them created great hostility. Ruben Archer Torrey, dean of the Los Angeles Bible Institute and one of the most prominent fundamentalists of the period, referred to the pentecostals as the "last vomit of Satan" (Quebedeaux, 1983). Torrey's rhetoric was extreme, but most fundamentalists violently rejected pentecostal practice. The hostility has continued into the present: The fundamentalist leader Jerry Falwell once stated that those who spoke in tongues had eaten too much pizza the night before, and Nancy Ammerman reported that in a fundamentalist congregation she studied, the pastor warned his parishioners that pentecostals "are allowing Satan to work in their lives" (1987, p. 81).

Why should seemingly minor differences in doctrine between two similar religious movements entail such hostility? There are several reasons. Most important, the doctrinal differences that may seem minor to those outside of the evangelical tradition are quite important to those within it. The fundamentalists insisted on an extreme, pure doctrine and rejected any deviations from those beliefs. For fundamentalists, salvation came through the saving grace of the **born-again experience.** Pentecostals believed in additional levels of grace, including a sanctifying grace of the baptism of the Holy Spirit. Issues such as salvation, grace, and the purity of doctrine are extremely important to evangelicals, and substantive disputes on these issues arouse much heat.

Second, both movements arose at approximately the same time and competed for roughly the same set of potential members. Fundamentalist pastors worried that they would lose their congregants to a pentecostal church and thus chose to demonize the competition to help fill their pews. Like competitors of all kinds, movement leaders chose to focus on the differences between fundamentalism and related religious movements rather than on their similarities, partly in an effort to differentiate their product and demonstrate its superiority.

Finally, there are differences in style that accompany these doctrinal distinctions and that persist today. Fundamentalists are a serious lot and believe that knowing God's will requires concentrated study of "the Book." Fundamentalist sermons are laced with Scripture: Pastors cite the text to support their themes and frequently tie together passages from several books and chapters of the Bible. Congregants read these passages along with the minister from their well-worn Bibles. In contrast, pentecostals worship through ecstatic outpourings of spiritual joy, and in their services people shout, jump, and occasionally fall onto the floor in religious ecstasy. One pentecostal outpouring in the United States entailed uncontrolled laughter, which swept the congregation and lasted for some time. Fundamentalists are uncomfortable with such exuberant worship.

It is small wonder, then, that the serious fundamentalist clergy worried that church members might be tempted to go down the street to the local pentecostal church. Yet the fundamentalists were initially far better situated to mobilize their congregations into politics, for their sermons linked the inspired word of God to events of the day. A pastor could preach a series of sermons on a political issue, weaving together divergent scriptural references to support his position, and could finally advocate political action with some accepted evidence that it was the will of God. In contrast, the imminent religious experience in pentecostal services had no obvious political meaning and thus was more difficult to mobilize. Early pentecostal churches focused on spiritual experience, not politics.

Thus, fundamentalists formed the backbone of Christian Right activity from the turn of the century through the mid-1980s. Only in recent years have pentecostals and charismatics moved into political action.

The Fundamentalist Political Revolt

The fundamentalist movement generated enormous energy and spawned the creation of many organizations. In the 1920s this energy spilled over into politics, as fundamentalist ministers began to challenge modernism head-on by defending the literal interpretation of the Genesis creation story against scientific theories. They objected to the teaching of evolution in high school classes and sought to remove evolution from the curriculum and replace it with the teaching of biblical creationism. Organizations such as the **Bible League of North America**, the **Bible Crusaders of America**, the **Defenders of the Christian Faith**, and an offshoot, the **Flying Fundamentalists**, which sent squadrons of speakers throughout the Midwest, all fought the teaching of evolution in public schools. State-level organizations formed as well and were active in many states.[6]

The antievolution groups used a variety of tactics in their efforts to pass state laws banning the teaching of evolution. Their leaders sought to meet with state legislators to persuade them of the validity of their positions, and other activists addressed large rallies in an effort to mobilize public opinion. This mixing of quiet persuasion and public pressure marked the antievolution crusades as one of the most sophisticated of the various waves of Christian Right activity.

Perhaps the movement's greatest asset was William Jennings Bryan, a frequent Democratic presidential candidate who held leftist-populist economic views but who had ties to the fundamentalist leadership. Bryan became convinced that German militarism was linked to the teachings of Darwin, and he invested much of his personal energies and reputation on behalf of the antievolution crusades. In leading the campaign, Bryan was fighting social Darwinism and, more important, the teachings of the German philosopher Nietzsche, which he believed had been the impetus for German expansion in World War I (Wills, 1990).

In all, thirty-seven antievolution bills were introduced in twenty state legislatures, but most failed to pass. One bill died in a committee on fish, game, and oysters—apparently referred there because the bill proscribed teaching that humans had evolved from lower organisms.[7] The climax of the antievolution crusades was the famous **Scopes trial,** in which William Jennings Bryan took the stand to defend the fundamentalist view of evolution, only to be humiliated by Clarence Darrow's questioning (see Box 2.1). Bryan died soon afterward, and the antievolution crusades lacked a prominent national leader (Lienesch, 1995).

Although the Scopes trial was widely interpreted as a defeat for the fundamentalist leadership, its outcome was more ambiguous. John Thomas Scopes was convicted of teaching evolution, but because of Darrow's efforts to attract great media attention to the trial, the conviction was quickly overturned by the state supreme court—a move that therefore denied Darrow an opportunity to appeal to the U.S. Supreme Court and set a national precedent. Moreover, many textbook publishers, fearing further controversy, removed references to evolution from biology texts soon after the Scopes case. Not until the Soviet Union launched the Sputnik satellite into space in 1957 did evolution again become a major component of high school biology classes, as Americans sought to catch up to the perceived Soviet lead in science and technology.

•••

BOX 2.1

The Great Monkey Trial

Journalists called it the "trial of the century," for it involved a clash of two strong men and, more important, of two strong ideas. In Dayton, Tennessee, John Thomas Scopes stood accused in 1925 of teaching evolution in the public schools. A state law banned the teaching of any doctrine that contradicted creationism, and modernists had encouraged Scopes to teach evolution to provide a test case of the constitutionality of the Tennessee law.

In the sweltering July heat in a time before air conditioning, more than 100 newspaper reporters crammed into the courtroom, leaving only for quick gulps of lemonade from the stands outside. By July 21 more than 3,000 onlookers crowded the aisles and stood huddled outside, listening to accounts carried back from those who stood just inside. A jury of twelve farmers listened carefully to the testimony and to the arguments of two of the era's biggest personalities.

Scopes was defended by Clarance Darrow, the premier trial lawyer of his day. Darrow was a longtime critic of creationism and a proponent of the philosophy of Nietzsche. William Jennings Bryan was a perennial Democratic presidential candidate who opposed the banks and monopolies and advocated inflating the currency to enable farmers and other debtors to pay off their loans with newspaper money. Although Bryan's economic views were more leftist than those of any major party candidate in history, he became one of the leading opponents of the teaching of evolution, perhaps because he thought Darwinism and Nietzsche's philosophy had inspired German militarism that led to World War I.

Bryan and Darrow had disliked each other for years, and Darrow had published in the *Chicago Tribune* a long list of questions to Bryan about the Bible designed to undermine the position of biblical literalism. Bryan agreed to prosecute the Scopes case in part because it gave him a chance to take on Darrow. It proved to be a disastrous decision.

Bryan was in poor health, whereas Darrow was fit and energetic. The trial climaxed when Darrow called Bryan to the stand and questioned him about his belief in the literal interpretation of the Bible. Under Darrow's sharp questionin, it became clear that Bryan had not thought carefully about many of the issues of biblical literalism, and in one portion of his testimony he angered fundamentalists by admitting that the earth may have been created over a period longer than six days.

Darrow scored points in other portions of the questioning as well. At two points, he focused in on apparent inconsistencies in the Bible. The following transcript omits some repetitive questioning but shows Bryan's difficulty.

Darrow: Did you ever discover where Cain got his wife?

....

Bryan:	No, Sir; I leave the agnostics to hunt for her.
Darrow:	You have never found out?
Bryan:	I have never tried to find out.
Darrow:	The Bible says he got one, doesn't it? Were there other people on the earth at that time?
Bryan:	I cannot say.
Darrow:	There were no others recorded, but Cain got a wife.
Bryan:	That is what the Bible says.
Darrow:	Where she came from, you do not know?
Darrow:	Do you think the sun was made on the fourth day?
Bryan:	Yes.
Darrow:	And they had evening and morning without the sun?
Bryan:	I believe it was creation as there told, and if I am not able to explain it I will accept it. Then you can explain it to suit yourself.

Many fundamentalists objected to the politicization of their movement, and eventually the crusade became limited to the most extreme fundamentalists, and funding became tight (Cole, 1931). As enthusiasm for antievolution activities waned, some fundamentalist leaders began to focus on a different message—anticommunism. Anticommunism was a natural rallying issue for fundamentalists, for many believed that the Bible predicted that the ultimate battle between the forces of Christ and the Antichrist would be fought in Israel, with the latter's forces coming from the land then occupied by the Soviet Union. Communism was a new force in the world in the 1920s, and its militant atheism resonated with this interpretation of Scripture.

During the Great Depression of the 1930s and into World War II, many fundamentalist organizations remained active, but their financial base eroded substantially. Some of their leaders drifted into fascism, anti-Semitism, and bigotry (Ribuffo, 1983). The fundamentalist Christian Right continued to preach anticommunism, but this theme lacked strong appeal in the depths of the Great Depression, and the organizations faded into obscurity.

In the aftermath of the Scopes trial and the failure of Prohibition, fundamentalists and other evangelicals retreated from politics in what has been called the "great reversal." Politics was seen as an ultimately futile endeavor. Yet during this period, fundamentalists built Bible colleges, churches, and new organizations, including the **American Council of Christian Churches** (ACCC). The ACCC was vehemently anticommunist, and its leadership even attacked leaders of mainline Protestant denominations for their alleged ties to communists. Its extremism alienated many moderate fundamentalists, who formed in 1942 the **National Association of Evangelicals** (NAE) and launched a movement that became known as **neoevangelicalism.** The neoevangelicals took orthodox doctrinal positions but were more moderate than the fundamentalists, both in religion and politics. Their religious moderation was evident in their rejection of separatism, their political moderation in their unwillingness to label their political opponents as communists.

The Anticommunist Crusades

After World War II, the Soviet Union emerged as the only serious international rival of the United States. A number of political figures began to stir fears of domestic communist influence. The most notable was Senator Joseph McCarthy of Wisconsin, who charged that much of America's government was infiltrated by communist agents. McCarthy's campaign helped establish a political market for anticommunist groups, and fundamentalist entrepreneurs formed a set of new political organizations to take part in the anticommunist movement. The **Christian Crusade**, the **Christian Anti-Communism Crusade**, and the **Church League of America** were all formed by leaders of the ACCC and emphasized primarily the threat of domestic communists.

Using radio broadcasts and traveling "schools of anticommunism," these groups focused narrowly on the "Red menace." These schools did not always emphasize the fundamentalist roots of the organizations and thus attracted not only highly religious fundamentalists who were recruited in churches but also secular anticommunists (Wolfinger et al., 1969; Wilcox, 1992). Regardless of their religious ties, those who attended the anticommunist schools were convinced that communists had infiltrated important national political institutions (Koeppen, 1969; Wolfinger et al., 1969).

The issue agenda was slightly broader than the one pursued by the antievolution groups of the 1920s. The Christian Anti-Communism Crusade officially opposed Medicare (labeling it socialized medicine) and sex education (arguing that it would weaken the nation's moral fiber and make America ripe for communist takeover). These issues were secondary to combating domestic communist infiltration, however, and were always linked directly to the communist conspiracy.

The fundamentalist anticommunist crusades never attracted a wide audience and were not well known even among those conservative fundamentalists most sympathetic to their message. McCarthy's crusade ended in disarray after he attacked the military, but the groups survived McCarthy's demise and signed on with enthusiasm to Barry Goldwater's 1964 presidential bid. After Goldwater's landslide defeat, the fundamentalist anticommunist groups slid into obscurity.[8]

Yet even as the Christian Right of the 1950s faded away, the religious conservatives who served as their target constituency continued to build infrastructure— Bible colleges, Christian bookstores, and specialized magazines and newspapers (Ammerman, 1987). One of the best-selling books of the 1970s was Hal Lindsey's *The Late Great Planet Earth*, which mixed premillennialism with far-right, often paranoid politics. Christian radio and television programs and stations began to proliferate, providing leading fundamentalist, pentecostal, and evangelical preachers a wider audience.

The late 1960s and early 1970s also brought rapid growth of the **charismatic** movement in mainline Protestant and Catholic churches. Like the pentecostals at the turn of the century, charismatics emphasized the importance of the "gifts of the Spirit," and many spoke in tongues or were slain in the Spirit. Unlike the pentecostals, however, the charismatics did not form their own churches but instead built an ecumenical movement across denominational lines and established charismatic caucuses within their home denominations. Charismatic businessmen's groups sprang up, and in many communities charismatic Catholics, Episcopalians, Methodists, Lutherans, and others met together in churches and other public places to worship. Some individual churches within mainline Protestant denominations adopted charismatic worship styles. The charismatics became an important source of support for Pat Robertson's 1988 presidential campaign.

The Fundamentalist Right of the 1980s

In the late 1970s, after a period of relative quiescence, a new fundamentalist Christian Right organized. Two sets of events seem to have precipitated this third wave of activity. First, a series of local political movements across the country demonstrated the potential political energy of fundamentalists and evangelicals in politics. Evangelicals rallied to protest textbooks used in the Kanawha County, West Virginia, public schools, to help repeal gay rights legislation in Dade County, Florida, and to oppose the Equal Rights Amendment (ERA) in many states and cities—in each case showing that evangelicals can be enthusiastic and effective political actors (Wald, 1992).

In 1976 the presidential candidacy of Jimmy Carter, a born-again Southern Baptist, provided more proof that evangelicals might be politicized. Carter, Democratic governor of Georgia, was a deeply religious man who had taught Sunday school for many years, and his sister was an evangelist. Carter publicly called on evangelicals to abandon their historical distrust of politics, and his campaign mobilized white evangelicals to vote in greater numbers than in past elections. When conservative leaders realized that fundamentalists and other evangelicals might be induced to become more involved in politics and that it might be possible to mold that political action into support of Republican candidates, they provided resources to help form groups such as the Moral Majority, the **Christian Voice**, and the **Religious Roundtable** in 1978 and 1979 (Guth, 1983; Wilcox, 1992; Moen, 1989).

Of all the fundamentalist groups of the 1970s and 1980s, the Moral Majority attracted the most attention. Its leader was Jerry Falwell, a Baptist Bible Fellowship pastor who had built the Thomas Road Baptist Church in Lynchburg, Virginia, from an initial gathering of thirty-five adults into a megachurch with more than 15,000 members.[9] Falwell's televised sermons were broadcast as the *Old Time Gospel Hour* and were carried on more than 300 stations. Falwell was an eager advocate for the Christian Right, appearing on television programs soon after the 1980 election to claim that evangelicals had provided Ronald Reagan's victory margin.

The Moral Majority built its organization primarily through pastors in the Baptist Bible Fellowship (BBF). Falwell recruited most of the organization's state and county leaders through the BBF, and this enabled him quickly to establish organizations in most states and in many counties (Liebman, 1983). When the media "discovered" the Christian Right in early 1981, the Moral Majority appeared on the surface to have a thriving organization.

These ready resources came with a price, however. The BBF pastors were religious entrepreneurs, and a pastor often built a church from scratch from a small circle of friends who first met in the pastor's living room. Many pastors hoped eventually to establish a megachurch as Falwell and some others had done. Most sought to build auxiliary organizations such as church schools. These men were frequently too busy with their religious construction to build a political organization.

Moreover, the BBF pastors were a generally intolerant lot. They were hostile to Catholics, pentecostals, charismatics, evangelicals, and mainline Protestants and not especially warm toward other Baptist churches. Their state Moral Majority organizations seldom had leaders outside of their faith, and those who did serve often felt uncomfortable and unwelcome. Not surprisingly, surveys of state Moral

Majority membership generally found a majority were Baptists and few, if any, were Catholics (Wilcox, 1992; Georgianna, 1989).

Thus, although the Moral Majority organization looked impressive on paper, in practice most state organizations were moribund (Hadden et al., 1987). The few state and local groups that were active went their considerably divergent ways, often to the embarrassment of the national organization. In Maryland, for example, the state organization made its stand on the issue of the sale by a beachfront bakery of "anatomically correct" cookies, which the organization labeled as pornographic. The incident attracted national media attention and ultimately succeeded in boosting cookie sales.

Christian Voice was formed around the same time by Robert Grant, initially from state-level antigay and antipornography groups in California. Pat Robertson provided some early funding for the group, which specialized in producing scorecards that rated the "moral votes" of members of Congress. Christian Voice established a few state chapters but remained primarily a national organization.

The Moral Majority, Christian Voice, and other groups of the 1970s and 1980s had a far broader issue agenda than their predecessors. The core agenda involved opposition to abortion, to civil rights protection for gays and lesbians, and to the ERA and support for school prayer and tuition tax credits for religious schools. But the organizations staked positions on a variety of other issues. Falwell made a highly publicized defense of South Africa and consistently supported increases in defense spending. The *Moral Majority Report*, the organization's newsletter, attempted to build support for conservative economic issues as well, including a subminimum wage, a return to the gold standard, and cuts in social welfare spending.

Although studies showed that the Moral Majority and other groups had the steady support of 10 to 15 percent of the public, their fortunes were more directly tied to the direct-mail revenues that funded the organizations. By the mid-1980s, it became increasingly harder for these groups to induce the primarily elderly women who constituted their financial base to part with their money.

This was true for two reasons. First, Reagan's reelection campaign in 1984 told these conservative Christians that it was already "morning in America," and the fuzzy Norman Rockwell images that were the core of Reagan's television advertising sent the message that his presidency had succeeded in restoring America to its historical values. Reagan's campaign and subsequent reelection made it appear less necessary to send money to "save" America.

Second, scandals involving televangelists in the latter part of the 1980s made many more people skeptical about the increasingly frequent appeals for money. Although these evangelists had not been political activists, their widely publicized problems hurt fundraising by the Moral Majority and damaged the presidential campaign of Pat Robertson. Jim Bakker was accused of various sexual and financial improprieties, and he eventually served time in prison for fraud. The investigations into Bakker's financial dealings revealed that he and his wife had provided their dog with an air-conditioned doghouse and had gold fixtures in their bathrooms. Oral Roberts's claim that God had threatened to "call him home" if his viewers did not contribute several million dollars to his ministry drew widespread ridicule. A Doonesbury cartoon noted that Roberts's claim, if true, would mean that God was a common terrorist using Roberts as a hostage to extort ransom.

All of this made it difficult for the Moral Majority to raise money through direct mail, and by 1988 it was strapped for cash. The organization was disbanded in 1989. Falwell claimed he quit because he had accomplished his goal, but the key issue agenda of the Moral Majority remained unrealized. Like the other fundamentalist crusades before it, the Moral Majority eventually folded its tent and went home. In late 1999, Falwell began to explore the possibility of creating another organization to replace the Moral Majority, although by spring of 2000 he had not formed a new group.

The Robertson Campaign

In 1987, Marion "Pat" Robertson announced that he would seek the Republican presidential nomination. Robertson was an ordained Baptist minister whose father had served as a Democratic senator from Virginia. Although Robertson had never held elected office, he had been active in Virginia politics for a decade and had built a highly successful business empire.

Robertson's *700 Club* television show was very different from Falwell's fundamentalist sermons. The program was a religious talk show, with a variety of guests sharing their music or testimony with Robertson and Ben Kenslow, his African-American cohost. Robertson also regularly provided a conservative analysis of political events in the news.

Robertson was a charismatic, and in the earliest shows he spoke in tongues and healed by faith. Although his later programs did not feature these religious gifts, his audience continued to include large numbers of pentecostals and charismatics. Robertson welcomed guests from many religious traditions, including Catholics, mainline Protestants, evangelicals, fundamentalists, pentecostals, charismatics, and black Protestants. Robertson himself noted his eclectic approach: "In terms of the succession of the church, I'm a Roman Catholic. As far as the majesty of worship, I'm an Episcopalian; as far as the belief in the sovereignty of God, I'm Presbyterian; in terms of holiness, I'm a Methodist; in terms of the priesthood of believers and baptism, I'm a Baptist; in terms of the baptism of the Holy Spirit, I'm a Pentecostal. So I'm a little bit of all of them."[10]

Robertson launched his campaign by gathering some 3 million signatures on petitions asking him to run, and these individuals served as the financial base of his campaign. Most of these contributors were regular viewers of his *700 Club* program, and many made regular gifts of $19.88 as part of the "1988 Club" (Brown, Powell, and Wilcox, 1995). Robertson's first campaign finance report to the Federal Election Commission contained the names of 70,000 donors and had to be delivered on a sixteen-foot truck.

Allen Hertzke (1993) described Robertson's campaign as a populist crusade to return America to a sound moral footing. Robertson decried the failures of the American education system, focusing not only on the teaching of secular humanism and the absence of school prayer but also on the failure of modern education methods to teach "the basics" effectively. He opposed abortion, which he argued was harmful because it reduced the number of babies born, thereby also reducing the number of potential taxpayers that could eventually pay for the retirements of the baby boomers. He touched briefly on the historical Christian Right theme of anticommunism, claiming that missiles were hidden in caves on Cuba, but he focused most of his campaign on domestic politics.

His economic positions were complex and did not fit neatly into the mainstream Republican debates between fiscal conservatives and supply-side economists. He strongly criticized the morality of large corporations that put profits ahead of morals and the world banking cartel, which he blamed for maintaining tight money that hurt working families. His most controversial stand was his call for a "Year of Jubilee," a year in which debt would be forgiven. Basing his proposal on an Old Testament account of a similar policy in ancient Israel, Robertson argued that the growing mountains of debt (both domestic and foreign) threatened to overwhelm the international economy. By calling for debt relief and looser money, Robertson echoed the earlier populist campaign of William Jennings Bryan but drew the ridicule of the *Wall Street Journal*.

Robertson's campaign got off to a good start. He probably won the first round of balloting in the early multistage Michigan caucus-convention, and he beat George Bush for second place in the Iowa caucuses.[11] But a disastrous series of stories undermined his campaign: He was forced to drop a suit in which he charged that an account of how his father kept him out of combat in the Korean War was libelous; journalists reported that his wife was very pregnant when they married; and Robertson claimed that he knew where the hostages were in Lebanon (though he had not shared that information with the government) and that there were secret missile bases in the caves of Cuba.

About the same time, televangelist Jimmy Swaggert was caught in a motel room with a prostitute, and television accounts reminded viewers of Jim Bakker's sex scandal and Oral Roberts's financial demands. Swaggert had supported Robertson, and Robertson initially blamed the scandal on a dirty trick of the Bush campaign, but it was soon revealed that a fellow televangelist had alerted the newspapers to Swaggert's escapades in revenge for an earlier episode in which Swaggert had accused him of sexual impropriety. Taken together, these stories all took a heavy toll.

Robertson's campaign also suffered from some of the religious prejudices that limited the appeal of the Moral Majority. Although he made efforts to reach out to Catholics and blacks, neither group voted often in Republican primaries. Moreover, fundamentalists were actually *less* likely than mainline Protestants to support Robertson, presumably because of disapproval of his pentecostal leanings. Studies revealed that Robertson's support was limited largely to charismatic and pentecostal Christians (Green and Guth, 1988; Wilcox, 1992; Brown, Powell, and Wilcox, 1995).

Robertson lost badly in the Super Tuesday primaries, including in Texas, where he outspent Bush by almost three to one. Ultimately, Robertson spent more money than any presidential candidate in history to that point to garner only thirty-five pledged delegates. Robertson failed to win a single primary and lost badly even in his home state of Virginia.

Yet the Robertson campaign was a vital part of the birth of a new, more sophisticated Christian Right. In many states where Bush won the Republican primary, Robertson's forces continued to work to select delegates to the convention. Ultimately, there were many delegates at the national convention who were pledged by state law to vote for Bush but who supported Robertson. More important, Robertson's Republicans worked to gain influence in and even control of state and local party committees.[12] These activists provided a core of skilled political workers ready to enlist in the next Christian Right crusade.

After Robertson's defeat and the disbanding of the Moral Majority, many observers proclaimed the Christian Right to be defeated, argued that its defeat had always been inevitable, and wrote its obituary.[13] In fact, research showed that support for the movement and its agenda had not declined, any more than it had surged in the early 1980s (Wilcox, 1992).

In 1989, Robertson launched the Christian Coalition. In June 1990, the Coalition took out a full-page ad in the *Washington Post* and other national newspapers warning members of Congress to vote against funding for the National Endowment for the Arts. The Coalition threatened to pass out 100,000 reproductions of controversial art by Robert Mapplethorpe and Andres Serrano in districts where members voted for funding. The text of the advertisement told of the kind of Coalition Robertson was trying to build. "There may be more homosexuals and pedophiles in your district than there are Roman Catholics and Baptists. You may find that the working folks in your district want you to use their tax money to teach their sons how to sodomize each other. You may find that the Roman Catholics in your district want their money spent on pictures of the Pope soaked in urine. **BUT MAYBE NOT.**" Robertson's clear appeal to Catholics and Baptists—two constituencies that did not rally to his presidential bid—signaled a conscious effort to build a broader, ecumenical Christian Right.

The Christian Right, 1920–1990: Continuity and Change

The waves of Christian Right activity between 1920 and 1990 had several things in common. Each was mobilized through infrastructure and communication channels already in place—the WCFA, the ACCC, the Baptist Bible Fellowship and Falwell's *Old Time Gospel Hour* and its contributor list, the *700 Club* and its list of donors. In each movement, anticommunism and education were important elements of the agenda, although they varied in importance.[14] Each was built around one or more preachers, who used the technology of the time (mass meetings, radio, television, direct mail) to reach an increasingly broader mass audience.

The first three waves of activity were based in the fundamentalist segment of the evangelical community, and each suffered because of the religious intolerance of fundamentalist leaders. None of the three fundamentalist movements succeeded in building an enduring or even significant grassroots presence, and all faded away when the initial enthusiasm died down. The Robertson campaign, however, made conscious appeals to a wide variety of Christians and even to conservative Jews, and the Christian Right of the 1990s has made substantial efforts to build a solid, interlocking network of grassroots organizations.

A Second Coming? The Christian Right, 1990–2000

At the end of the 1980s, the Christian Right seemed defeated. Most of the major organizations that had been active in that decade were disbanded or moribund, and the conservative direct-mail industry was crowded and in disarray (Moen, 1994). Yet even as the large national organizations died, movement activists planned a grassroots mobilization of immense scope. The goal was to have activists in place in every precinct in America by the millennium and to influence and perhaps control the Republican candidate-selection process. By the end of the decade, it was clear that this goal would not be achieved, and some observers were again proclaiming the end of the movement.

The most visible of the new organizations has been the Christian Coalition. Its former executive director, Ralph Reed, wrote of the need for a new ecumenicism in the movement and has appealed directly for conservative Catholics, Jews, and African Americans to join the coalition (Reed, 1994b). The Coalition made a conscious effort to build its state and county chapters around political activists, not preachers, in order to attract members from many religious traditions. The organization has distributed materials and held training sessions on how different religious groups can work and play well together. Other new organizations, including Focus on the Family and the Family Research Council, are discussed in more detail in chapter 3.

The Christian Coalition and other organizations of the 1990s initially had considerable success in building grassroots organizations. There were at one time county chapters in forty counties in Virginia, for example, and many counties had regional or other smaller chapters in place as well. The ultimate goal—to have organizations in every precinct in America—was never achieved, but these organizations did establish an important presence.

The Coalition and other new groups also had considerable success in forging ecumenical ties. In Virginia, the state Christian Coalition leader for a time was a Catholic (Bendyna, 1995), and in many other states Catholics and mainline Protestants have served as county chairs. Concerned Women for America had strong support among conservative Catholics in the northern part of the Virginia.

Whereas the Christian Right of the 1980s practiced confrontation, the new organizations have used different tactics. Originally, some Christian Coalition candidates ran as **stealth candidates,** hiding their ties with the organization. This brought complaints not only from liberals, who labeled the practice deception, but also from some conservative Christians, who charged that the tactic made it appear that Christians were afraid to profess their faith publicly. A Pennsylvania Christian Coalition manual that encouraged stealth candidacies was widely distributed and reprinted in the media, much to the discomfort of the organization's leaders, who argued that the manual was only a draft prepared by an overzealous volunteer.

More recently, the Christian Right has encouraged its activists and candidates to couch their arguments differently for religious and nonreligious audiences. Activists are told to "mainstream the message" by avoiding explicitly religious language in public speeches and by emphasizing positions on taxes, crime, abortion, and gay rights. Although many liberals complain that this tactic is just another form of a stealth candidacy, Christian Right activists respond that all candidates tailor their message to different audiences. Michael Farris, longtime movement activist and director of a group that provides legal protection to homeschool parents, noted:

"Evangelical Christians need to find ways to communicate effectively with different people. They can't just interact among themselves. Many are learning that as they interact in the Republican party, not everyone understands or accepts the lingo that evangelicals use when talking to each other. . . . I've got to understand the other person if I want to be persuasive. Understanding that person means respecting that other person. I've got to get around other people's mental roadblocks. That means respecting where that person is coming from. That's the way that evangelical Christians can be more effective. It's a growing up thing. That is, being able to disagree with others but still be respectful of their values. That's the trick. Not all of our spokesmen have been very effective at that."[15]

As part of their efforts to adopt the secular language of politics, Christian Right candidates and activists have couched their political arguments in the "rights" language of liberalism (Moen, 1992). Instead of arguing that America is a Christian nation and therefore public schools should begin with a Christian prayer, activists now argue that Christian children have a right to exercise their religious beliefs freely in prayer. Instead of arguing that certain textbooks endorse evil lifestyles, activists now talk of "parental rights" in helping mold their children's education. Abortion is framed as involving the rights of the unborn. The substantive solution to these infringements of the asserted rights is identical to those policies advocated by earlier incarnations of the Christian Right, but the justification for those policies is markedly different.

Moreover, many Christian Right activists and candidates have adopted the language of victimization. Although conservatives have long decried efforts by African Americans, women, and gays and lesbians to portray themselves as victims of discrimination, Christian conservatives now use this same language. In a Virginia lieutenant governor's race in 1993, Don Beyer, Democratic candidate, attacked Michael Farris's ties to the Christian Right. Farris responded by charging that Beyer was practicing bigotry against religious citizens. Farris's attack drew widespread media attention and has been copied by other Christian Right candidates.

Like the Moral Majority, the Christian Coalition and other groups of the 1990s have a wide policy agenda that includes domestic policy positions on health care reform, taxes, and crime, but the issues of primary concern to most activists are abortion, education, and a constellation of issues relating to families and sexuality. Yet the Christian Right groups of the 1990s are more clearly political organizations than their predecessors, and they attract a more eclectic set of activists with varying sets of policy concerns.

Many of these activists are also members of local organizations that stress a somewhat different set of issues. The large national organizations frequently provide resources to local activists to form small local groups and help coordinate the efforts of this network of local organizations. Because these groups usually emphasize local issues, they serve as a valuable recruiting mechanism for the Christian Right.

The Christian Right moving into the twenty-first century was far more effective than the organizations that came before it. Matthew Moen, a political scientist, was among the first to write of this transformation: "The Christian Right became a more sophisticated political player. . . by virtue of its early leaders gaining some experience in politics, and by the infusion of politically adept newcomers to supplement (or supplant) the 'old guard'" (Moen, 1992, p. 3).

Near the end of the 1990s, two developments undermined much of the progress that the movement had made early in the decade. First, the largest national organization faltered. The Christian Coalition lost momentum when Ralph Reed, a savvy political operative with a Ph.D. in history, resigned as executive director and hung out his shingle as a political consultant. His departure destabilized the organization, which had depended on Reed's keen ear for politics to offset Robertson's tendency to extreme rhetoric and unexpected proclamations. After Reed's departure, Robertson played a far more active role in the organization.

Ironically, it was Robertson's moderation that led to a series of key resignations by national, state, and local leaders. In late 1998 and again in early 1999, Robertson proclaimed that a ban on abortions was not achievable and that the Coalition should work to limit abortions through additional restrictions and bans on certain late-term procedures. More importantly, in February 1999, Robertson called for an end to efforts to remove Bill Clinton from the presidency. Although Robertson was primarily acknowledging political reality, many activists believed that they had been betrayed—that the Coalition had asked them to commit their resources to removing the president, only to abandon that effort with no warning.

The decline of the Christian Coalition may or may not be permanent and will be explored in more detail later in the book. In the short run, it has created an opportunity for competing social movement organizations, which have attempted to recruit some of the Coalition's activists.

A second, and more potentially important, development is the emergence of a debate among some longstanding movement activists over whether political action is effective. In 1999, as the impeachment effort stalled, Paul Weyrich, a long-time conservative activist who helped form the Moral Majority, announced that the culture war was lost and advised conservative Christians to begin to create alternative cultural institutions and to withdraw from the culture. Two former Moral Majority activists, Cal Thomas and Ed Dobson, argued in a highly publicized book, *Blinded by Might*, that the evangelicals had been seduced by the lure of political power and that they should return to their primary mission of saving souls.

The Target Constituency of the Christian Right

The Christian Coalition, Focus on the Family, and Concerned Women for America are all social movement organizations seeking to mobilize members of their potential constituency. Like all social movements, they seek to build a common identity, a common set of complaints, a shared belief that the constituency has been unfairly treated by society, and support for collective action. Two important factors that determine whether the organizations fail or succeed are how effectively they mobilize their base and whether they can expand beyond that core constituency.

Most analysts agree that the principal target audience of the Christian Right remains the white evangelical community. In addition, the contemporary Christian Right is clearly targeting conservative Catholics, mainline Protestants, and African Americans.

White Evangelicals

White evangelicals are united by a common core of theology: They share a belief in the importance of a personal conversion experience that involves repenting of sin and accepting Jesus Christ as personal savior. Most, though not all, evangelical churches refer to this experience as being "born again."[16] They also agree that the Bible is the inerrant word of God and that Christians should spread their witness and seek to convert others to the faith. Yet evangelicals are also divided by their doctrine, especially on how to interpret the Bible and on how the Holy Spirit operates in their lives.

We might conceive of evangelicals as the broad set of individuals who share the core doctrinal beliefs and of fundamentalists, pentecostals, and charismatics as subsets of evangelicals. Those evangelicals who do not belong to any of these groups are often referred to as "other evangelicals."[17]

Fundamentalists, pentecostals, charismatics, and other evangelicals can be identified in survey data in different ways, and these variations often account for the sometimes conflicting claims made about evangelicals. All groups except charismatics can be identified by the denominations they attend. Those who attend Assembly of God churches are pentecostals, and those who go to Baptist Bible Fellowship churches can be classified as fundamentalists. A denominational definition of evangelicalism helps us focus on the historical and social basis for the movement and on how different denominations have splintered and merged around various interpretations of doctrine.

A denominational definition has the advantage that many national and regional surveys ask a question about church affiliation, and thus we can compare evangelicals with other citizens quite easily. Moreover, because these questions have been asked for many years, we can trace the political behavior of evangelicals. Yet a denominational definition is less useful for identifying the theological subgroups among evangelicals. Many fundamentalists attend nondenominational churches, and charismatics are found in all mainline Protestant denominations and among Catholics as well. Some denominations, such as the Southern Baptists, are difficult to classify, since they continue to experience an internal struggle for control between the fundamentalists and neoevangelicals.

Moreover, many liberal denominations contain theologically conservative congregations. I grew up in the Walnut Grove United Methodist Church in West Virginia. Any denominational coding would place the liberal Methodists with mainline Protestants, but Walnut Grove was and remains an evangelical church, and most of its members would call themselves fundamentalists.

It is also possible to identify evangelicals by their doctrine, as noted by Lyman Kellstedt: "The predominant emphasis of evangelicalism is *doctrine*. It is 'right' doctrine that self-defined evangelicals look for when they 'check out' a person's Christian credentials" (Kellstedt, 1989, p. 29). The most frequent questions used to identify evangelicals ask if the respondents have been born again and assess their views of the Bible. Some surveys ask about the practice of spiritual gifts such as speaking in tongues. These measures have the strength of identifying evangelicals in all denominations, although many individuals claim to embrace evangelical doctrine yet exhibit only a marginal attachment to religion.[18]

Finally, some surveys identify evangelicals by inviting them to identify themselves. They ask Americans whether they consider themselves to be evangelicals, fundamentalists, charismatics, and/or pentecostals, in some case allowing only one positive response, in others allowing respondents to select multiple identities.

FIGURE 2.1

White Evangelical Religious Traditions

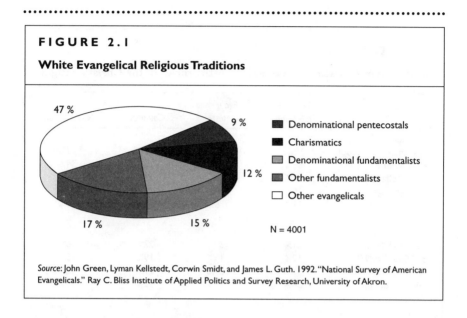

Source: John Green, Lyman Kellstedt, Corwin Smidt, and James L. Guth. 1992. "National Survey of American Evangelicals." Ray C. Bliss Institute of Applied Politics and Survey Research, University of Akron.

Such direct questions have the advantage of helping us understand what citizens mean by these terms, but they also reveal considerable confusion among Americans as to which terms might apply to their beliefs. [19]

Although these various measurements yield somewhat different subgroup results, white evangelicals constitute approximately a quarter of the public. Figure 2.1 begins with all whites who attend churches in evangelical denominations and then divides them into categories based on their denomination, their religious doctrine and identity. The data understate somewhat the number of charismatics, who can be found among other religious traditions as well.[20] These data show that about a third of white evangelicals are fundamentalists, and more than a fifth are pentecostals or charismatics.

Evangelicals differ from other Americans in some important ways. Table 2.1 shows some of the social characteristics of whites who attend mainline Protestant, evangelical Protestant, and Catholic churches and of those who profess no religious affiliation. White evangelicals are less likely than other whites to have a college degree and more likely to have failed to finish high school. These differences are not enormous, and they do not mean that all evangelicals are poorly educated. In the 1996 National Election Study data, nearly half of white evangelicals attended some college, although this figure is a bit higher than in other comparable studies. But evangelicals are one-third less likely than white Catholics or white mainline Protestants to have a college degree, and more likely than members of

TABLE 2.1

Social Characteristics of Potential Constituencies of the Christian Right

	Mainline Protestants	Evangelical Protestants	Catholics	No Affiliation
Education				
Less than high school	9%	18%	13%	13%
High school	36%	34%	29%	34%
Some college	25%	27%	27%	27%
College degree	20%	14%	21%	16%
Post-graduate	11%	6%	10%	11%
Family income				
Less than $19,000	21%	32%	22%	36%
$20,000–$29,999	12%	19%	19%	15%
$30,000–$39,999	31%	27%	27%	20%
$40,000 and up	36%	21%	32%	29%
Region				
Northeast	11%	5%	26%	11%
Midwest	39%	26%	33%	27%
South	37%	50%	22%	24%
West	13%	19%	27%	38%
Sex				
Female	62%	59%	50%	45%
Age				
18–30	14%	19%	17%	26%
31–45	32%	35%	36%	36%
46–60	20%	24%	20%	20%
61 and up	34%	23%	27%	19%
Religion				
Religion provides a good deal of guidance	36%	48%	31%	8%
Reads Bible daily	12%	24%	6%	3%
Prays several times a day	27%	43%	25%	5%
Attends church more than weekly	8%	22%	11%	0%

Source: 1996 National Election Study: Whites only.

these groups not to have finished high school. The income gap is somewhat wider, in part because evangelicals are more likely to live in families with a single wage-earner. Evangelicals are also more likely than other whites to live in the South. They are younger than mainline Protestants and Catholics but older than their more secular counterparts. Although surveys usually show that evangelicals are disproportionately female, this was not true in the 1996 National Election Study data.

There are important differences as well in the levels of religiosity. Evangelicals are more likely than white mainline Protestants or Catholics to indicate that religion provides a good deal of guidance in their lives. They attend church, pray, and read their Bible more often than other white Christians.[21] For many evangelicals, their church is their primary social network, and most of their friends attend the same church (Ammerman, 1987).

Evangelicals hold more traditional values and are more likely to take conservative positions on social issues. Table 2.2 shows the values and social issue positions of whites who attend mainline Protestant, evangelical Protestant, and Catholic churches and of those with no religious affiliation. Evangelicals are much more likely than all other whites to say that people should not be tolerant of those who choose to live by different moral values, and they are much more likely to indicate that belief in God is a very important prerequisite to being a good American. Evangelicals are not significantly different from other white Americans in their support of family values, or for equality.

Evangelicals are distinctively conservative on many social issues. They are more likely than other whites to oppose all abortions, and less likely to approve of them under all circumstances. More than 10 percent say they are certain that abortion should never be allowed, and that it is extremely important that it be prohibited. Yet note that more evangelicals support abortion under all circumstances than oppose it always: a majority of evangelicals support abortions under some but not all circumstances (Cook, Jelen, and Wilcox, 1992).

Evangelicals are also markedly less likely than other whites to support civil rights for gays and lesbians. More than half oppose laws banning discrimination against gays and lesbians, and nearly half oppose allowing gays and lesbians to serve in the military. They are also slightly more conservative than other Americans on women's roles, especially within families. White evangelicals are four times as likely as all other whites to indicate that men should have more power than women in families, although only a minority take that position.

Differences on other issues are far smaller, however. Table 2.3 shows issue positions of white religious groups on economic, foreign policy, race, and crime issues. In 1996 evangelicals are not distinctive on defense spending, although

TABLE 2.2

Political Values and Social-Issue Positions of White Religious Groups

	Mainline Protestants	Evangelical Protestants	Catholics	No Affiliation
Values				
Fewer problems if more family values	53%	67%	47%	32%
Don't tolerate those with different values	28%	41%	19%	12%
Belief in God very important for true Americans*	63%	85%	66%	37%
Worry less about equality	55%	57%	53%	53%
Social/Moral Issues				
Abortion				
Never allowed	5%	18%	13%	7%
Always allowed	45%	24%	36%	63%
Never allowed, certain, extremely important	2%	11%	6%	4%
No gay antidiscrimination laws	39%	53%	28%	28%
No gays in military	29%	47%	24%	30%
No gay adoption*	69%	86%	70%	61%
Women not have equal role	13%	17%	6%	7%
Mothers with young children should not work outside home	42%	50%	41%	34%
Men should have more power in families*	6%	21%	5%	3%
School prayer				
Chosen prayer	8%	14%	7%	5%
General prayer	22%	23%	26%	20%
Moment of silence	61%	58%	53%	47%

*indicates data from the 1992 NES.
Source: 1996 National Election Study.

other surveys have shown them more supportive of substantial military budgets. They are more likely than other whites to favor limits on immigration. On economic issues, white evangelicals are indistinguishable from mainline Protestants but more conservative than Catholics or those with no religious ties, despite

TABLE 2.3

Other Issue Positions of White Religious Groups

	Mainline Protestants	Evangelical Protestants	Catholics	No Affiliation
Foreign/Defense Issues				
More defense spending	42%	38%	30%	32%
Decrease number of immigrants a lot	27%	35%	25%	32%
Economic Issues				
Spend less on services	43%	45%	37%	38%
Spend less on food stamps	52%	52%	45%	46%
Spend less on homeless	15%	13%	9%	11%
Race/Crime Issues				
Government should not help blacks	60%	67%	58%	53%
Strongly favor death penalty	63%	70%	60%	63%
Oppose handgun control	52%	66%	47%	50%

Source: 1996 National Election Study.

their lower average incomes. Evangelicals are less likely to favor government aid to blacks, but more likely to support the death penalty and to oppose gun control—in each case primarily because evangelicals are disproportionately southern.

Yet this does not mean that white evangelicals are uniformly conservative. Abortion, gay rights, women's roles, and welfare divide the evangelical community as they do the rest of the nation. Although nearly half of white evangelicals strongly oppose allowing gays and lesbians to serve openly in the military, for example, more than four in ten favor lifting the ban. Moreover, although more than one in six evangelicals in 1996 opposed abortion under all circumstances, almost one in four favored allowing abortions in all circumstances.

This suggests that the Christian Right can attract its broadest support among evangelicals by taking positions that are moderately conservative—allowing abortions under a few circumstances, favoring a moment of silence instead of spoken prayer in the classroom, and avoiding any endorsement of gender inequality. Yet

TABLE 2.4

Selected Values and Issues: White and Black Evangelicals

	White Core	Other White	Black
Strongly Agree:			
Few problems if family values	84%	59%	52%
Don't tolerate those with			
different values	53%	32%	17%
Worry less about equality	60%	56%	45%
Abortion never allowed	40%	10%	18%
No gay antidiscrimination			
laws	64%	49%	29%
No gays in military	66%	39%	28%
Chosen school prayer	16%	11%	18%
General prayer	23%	22%	16%
Mothers with children should never			
work outside home	60%	14%	40%
Spend less on food stamps	64%	48%	23%

Source: 1996 National Election Study.

these positions may also fail to motivate the most ardent activists, who generally take quite conservative positions on these issues.

Within the white evangelical community is a smaller subset of Americans who might be called "core evangelicals." Core evangelicals attend evangelical churches once a week or more, profess a born-again experience, hold that the Bible is the inerrant word of God, and constitute the target activist base for the Christian Right. Whereas white denominational evangelicals constitute approximately one quarter of the population, this core group is much smaller—less than 9 percent of the general public. But the data in Table 2.4 show that this core group is significantly more conservative than other white evangelicals. A preponderance of core white evangelicals strongly agree that the country would have fewer problems if it had stronger family values, and more than half believe that we should not tolerate those with different values. Nearly two thirds oppose anti-discrimination laws for gays and lifting the ban to permit gays and lesbians to serve openly in the military.

Conservative Catholics

Although conservative Catholics did not feel welcome in the Moral Majority, the contemporary Christian Right later made special appeals to them (Bendyna, Green, Rozell, and Wilcox, 2000). There has long been a Catholic Right in America, and some Catholics rallied to the antievolution crusades and to Joseph McCarthy's anticommunism. Catholics were the principal audience for Father Charles Coughlin's ultraconservative radio broadcasts in the 1930s and later were a core element in the John Birch Society.

It is clear that many Catholics support some of the key issues of the Christian Right. The data in Table 2.2 show that significant minorities of Catholics support Christian Right positions on social issues. The principal issue the Christian Right relies on to win Catholic members is abortion. Catholics are also attracted to the movement's support of Christian schools, its general position that family values and Christian faith should be more prominent in public life, and, to a lesser extent, by issues such as homeschooling and opposition to gay rights.

Yet despite clear teachings by the Roman Catholic Church, only a minority of Catholics are strictly pro-life. Moreover, Catholics are more supportive than evangelicals of programs to aid the needy and of civil liberties protection for unpopular groups, and the church is officially opposed to the death penalty. It seems unlikely, therefore, that the Christian Right can ever hope to win the support of a majority of Catholics for its broad agenda.

Yet the Christian Right need not attract a majority of Catholics to be a formidable political force. If it were to attract a majority of white evangelicals, a sizable minority of white Catholics and mainline Protestants, and a credible number of black evangelicals, it would be a vital force in American politics.

In October 1995 the Christian Coalition announced the formation of the **Catholic Alliance**, a unit designed to attract Catholic members. The Catholic Alliance later severed its ties with the Christian Coalition and has been generally unsuccessful in building a social movement organization.

White Mainline Protestants

Although the Christian Coalition seldom mentions mainline Protestants as a target for future mobilization, Ralph Reed is a Presbyterian and Oliver North, Reagan White House official and Virginia Senate candidate, attends a charismatic Episcopal church. There are morally conservative Christians in Presbyterian, Methodist, Lutheran, and Episcopal churches across America, and some already have joined the Christian Right. Many hold orthodox doctrinal views, and some regularly watch televangelists, who provide some of their political cues.

Overall, however, mainline Protestants are quite moderate on social and moral issues. A clear majority favor abortion on demand, allowing gays and lesbians to serve openly in the military, and laws to prohibit job discrimination against homosexuals. Mainline Protestants are as conservative as evangelicals on economic issues (principally because of their relative affluence), but it is unlikely that a majority will enlist in a conservative moral crusade.

But the data in Table 2.2 show that a substantial majority of mainline Protestants do believe in family values and a moment of silence for voluntary school prayer, and more than half favor some restrictions on abortion. Earlier surveys show that a large majority favor parental notification on abortion. These views suggest that there may be room for some mobilization by Christian Right groups that take relatively moderate positions on key issues and stress abstract family values.

Black Evangelicals

A majority of African Americans are evangelicals, measured by either denomination or doctrine. A clear majority attend Baptist churches, believe that the Bible is the inerrant word of God, and report a born-again experience. Substantial numbers of blacks have had the spiritual experiences that are the core of pentecostal and charismatic Christianity as well. Moreover, blacks practice their religion: they attend church, read their Bibles, and pray more often than whites.

Yet these doctrinal beliefs and religious experiences do not translate into the same political orientations as for whites. Although African Americans and whites read from the same Bible, the meaning of the text is socially constructed in different ways in the two traditions. Most black churches interpret the Bible as a book of liberation, equality, and social compassion. Thus, black evangelicals are more likely than their white counterparts to oppose all forms of discrimination and to favor social programs to help the poor.

Yet many African-American evangelicals are quite conservative on moral issues, including gay rights, abortion, and school prayer, and this group would seem to constitute a potential constituency for the Christian Right. Many Christian Right leaders clearly perceive the potential, for Ralph Reed and others frequently lace their speeches with quotations from Martin Luther King Jr. and often compare their movement with the civil rights movement of the 1960s.

The data in Table 2.4 also contain selected attitudes of black evangelicals. The data suggest that a significant minority of black Protestants oppose abortion and favor prayer in public schools. Yet black Protestants are far more supportive of gay rights than white evangelicals and are markedly more liberal on economic, crime, and race issues.

There are two important barriers to mobilizing blacks into the Christian Right. First, blacks are overwhelmingly Democratic, and the Christian Right is active almost exclusively in the Republican party. In the 1996 National Election Study, only 3 percent of blacks identified as Republicans, with an additional 4 percent calling themselves independents who leaned toward the GOP. Fully 80 percent either identified as Democrats or leaned toward that party. If the Christian Right chose to pursue a bipartisan strategy, they might win black support for primary election candidates who took relatively conservative positions on social and moral issues, but even charismatic black **social conservatives** like Alan Keyes or J. C. Watts are unlikely to sway significant numbers of blacks to vote for Republicans.

The second major barrier is the Christian Right economic agenda. Most African-American evangelicals support government welfare programs, affirmative action, and a progressive income tax. Thus, when Christian Right leaders talk of abortion and school prayer, they may reach a receptive audience in some segments of the African-American community. But when they endorse a flat tax and an end to government welfare and affirmative action programs, they are likely to find few black supporters.

In 1997, the Christian Coalition launched a highly publicized initiative to engage black evangelicals into the movement. Called the Samaritan Project, the initiative sought to mobilize African Americans behind a program of school vouchers (called Hope and Opportunity Scholarships), school prayer, and stricter divorce laws, along with other programs. The Coalition dropped the Samaritan Project in 1999 as its budget deficit grew.

Putting It All Together:
Issue Groups in the Target Constituency

How likely is it that the Christian Right might make significant gains among white and black evangelicals, white mainline Protestants, and white Catholics? Tables 2.2 and 2.3 show only the percentage of each constituency group holding conservative positions on each concrete issue; they do not show the *packages* of issues in each religious community. Although we can see in Table 2.2 that 18 percent of white evangelicals take a strict pro-life position and 17 percent oppose gender equality for women, we cannot tell from those data whether these conser-

vative responses come from the same or different people. It may be that 17 percent of white evangelicals oppose both abortion and gender equality, or it may be
that 35 percent hold one or the other of these two positions. Most likely, the truth
is in between.

We can identify those people who hold similar sets of positions using the statistical technique of cluster analysis. In 1992 there were five different issue groupings
among members of the four main constituency groups for the Christian Right—
white evangelicals, mainline Protestants, Catholics, and black evangelicals. Individuals in the first issue group might be called "consistent conservatives," who are
quite conservative on basic values, social and moral issues, and defense issues and
generally conservative on economic and racial issues. The second group can be labeled "social conservatives." Its members are especially conservative on issues of
gay rights and also conservative on abortion and women's roles in the family.
They are much less conservative on women's roles in society, however, and are
moderately conservative on other issues.

The third group can be labeled "economic conservatives." These people are
generally moderate on all issues except economics, where they favor deep cuts in
social welfare spending, cuts in taxes, and efforts to balance the budget. The
fourth group might be labeled "values conservatives." These Americans take conservative positions on basic values and support a moment of silence on school
prayer but are otherwise moderate to liberal on social, economic, foreign policy
and defense, and race issues. Finally, individuals in the fifth group are consistently
liberal on all issues.

Of these five groups, the consistent conservatives and social conservatives are
the most likely converts to the Christian Right. Economic conservatives tend to be
moderate to liberal on social issues and so are unlikely to join a movement that
centers on conservative positions on social and moral concerns. Values conservatives might agree with Christian Right leaders that religion should play a larger
role in American public life and that family values are important, but they disagree sharply with the political platform of the Christian Right. Liberals are likely
to oppose the Christian Right at every turn. The values conservatives and liberals
combine to be a sizable bloc that supports liberal policy.

Figure 2.2 shows the alignment of each of the four main constituency groups
of the Christian Right within these five issue groupings. Among white evangelicals, a clear majority are either consistent conservatives or social conservatives.
This suggests that there is solid potential for the Christian Right to enlist many
evangelicals in its movement. Fully 30 percent fall into the liberal and values conservative groups, however, so this potential has clear limits. Among white mainline Protestants, white Catholics, and black evangelicals, the consistent and social

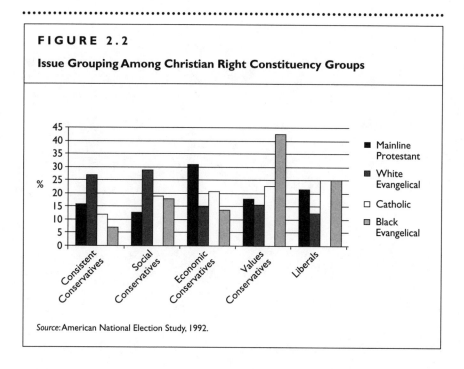

FIGURE 2.2

Issue Grouping Among Christian Right Constituency Groups

Legend:
- Mainline Protestant
- White Evangelical
- Catholic
- Black Evangelical

Categories: Consistent Conservatives, Social Conservatives, Economic Conservatives, Values Conservatives, Liberals

Source: American National Election Study, 1992.

conservatives issue groups are outnumbered by members of the two most liberal groupings. Between a quarter and a third fall into the two groupings that are most likely to support the Christian Right, however. This suggests that there is potential for the Christian Right to broaden its support beyond evangelical Christians. We will return to the question of the potential for the Christian Right in chapter 5.

Conclusion

Although there are potential supporters for the Christian Right among several different religious constituencies, there is opposition to its social agenda in all groupings as well. Clearly, groups such as the Christian Coalition do not speak for all Christians or even for all white evangelicals, but their social issue agenda does have appeal to many conservatives. If the Christian Right were to mobilize those potential constituents fully, they would be a powerful movement in American politics.

Well-organized social movement organizations exist that seek to mobilize these potential activists. The next chapter introduces the groups.

FIGURE 2.2
Issue Grouping Among Christian Right Constituency Groups

3

The Christian Right in American Politics

Think like Jesus. . . Fight like David. . . Lead like Moses. . . Run like Lincoln.

—Christian Coalition motto

ALTHOUGH THE CHRISTIAN RIGHT MOVEMENTS of the 1920s, 1950s, and 1980s all sought to influence public policy, the contemporary Christian Right is a far more sophisticated movement that pursues a variety of strategies to achieve a variety of goals. The Christian Right seeks to influence Republican nominations and to influence or control the party apparatus, to help the Republicans control the White House and Congress, to achieve legislative victories in Congress and state legislatures, to influence decisions by the U.S. Supreme Court, to win control of school boards in order to influence school curricula, and to win referenda in states and counties to implement parts of its agenda. Movement leaders are very ambitious, and their multi-front initiative is clearly the most sweeping in the history of American Christian conservatism.

In this chapter I first describe the key organizations of the contemporary Christian Right and discuss the special role that each plays in the movement. I then focus on the various political activities of the Christian Right and assess their impact.

The Christian Right in the 1990s

To understand the activities of the Christian Right, it is first necessary to identify the key actors in the movement. Although it is relatively easy to identify the most important national organizations, defining the precise boundaries of the Christian Right is more difficult. Moreover, much of the action in the 1990s was by state and even local organizations that may lack ties to national groups.

Many organizations were active in conservative Christian politics in the 1990s, but four stand out as the largest, most professional, and best organized. The Christian Coalition, Focus on the Family, **Family Research Council**, and Concerned Women for America have built sophisticated infrastructure to mobilize and inform their members and have active state and local affiliates.

The Christian Coalition

The most visible organization of the Christian Right is the Christian Coalition. Founded in 1989 from the detritus of the Pat Robertson campaign, the coalition once claimed a membership of 2.8 million members and supporters and 2,000 local chapters formed in all fifty states. Membership estimates provided by the organization have always been exaggerated, and many observers estimate that the organization's membership has dropped to fewer than 1 million, perhaps fewer than 500,000. In late 1999 the organization had organizations on paper in fifty states, but only seven were active (Goodstein, 1999).

In the middle of the 1990s, the organization's goal was to identify 10 million pro-family voters and to place neighborhood coordinators in each of the nation's 175,000 precincts by the turn of the century. In 1999, the Coalition announced a new strategy to reach out to churchgoing families and to recruit 100,000 church liaisons. In addition, the Coalition set an ambitious fundraising goal of $21 million to help retire the organization's large debt.

The Christian Coalition seeks to mold a truly inclusive religious Right. Its 1999 convention featured Catholic, Jewish, and African-American speakers, all of whom received an enthusiastic reception from the crowd. Workshops have in the past focused on building evangelical-Catholic alliances and on expanding support among Hispanics and African Americans. These highly visible, explicit efforts to broaden the base are a key part of the Christian Coalition agenda.

The organization's leader is Pat Robertson, a Baptist minister, television host, businessman, and former presidential candidate. Robertson is the author of a number of books, and his writings have attracted attention for their emphasis on strange conspiracies that include international bankers, the Trilateral Commission, and the Illuminati, a seventeenth-century offshoot of the Masons. Robertson's writings and speeches are frequently controversial and confrontational. He once predicted a hurricane would strike Orlando, Florida, because of its support for gay rights, and he has called for the assassination of hostile foreign heads of state (Jacoby, 1999).

The organization's first executive director, Ralph Reed, played the voice of moderation to Robertson's extremism. Reed frequently compared the Christian Coalition to the African-American civil rights movement, and once asked Christian Coalition activists at a national meeting to sign a card containing a series of pledges drafted by the Reverend Martin Luther King Jr. for the Southern Christian Leadership Conference, a religiously based civil rights group. (See Box 3.1).

After Reed resigned to launch a political consulting firm, the Coalition first split his responsibilities between Donald Hodel from the Family Research Council and Randy Tate, former member of Congress from Washington state. Tate resigned after serving a stint as the organization's lobbyist; Hodel resigned after clashing with Robertson over the organization's goals and strategies. The group has several vice presidents, most prominently Roberta Coombs, who formerly headed the South Carolina chapter of the organization.

. . . .

BOX 3.1

The Christian Coalition Pledge Card

---

1. Meditate daily on the teachings and life of Jesus.
2. Remember always that the movement seeks justice and reconciliation—not victory.
3. Walk and talk in the manner of love, for God is love.
4. Pray daily to be used by God so that all men might be free.
5. Observe with both friend and foe the ordinary rules of courtesy.
6. Seek to perform regular service for others and for the world.
7. Refrain from the violence of fist, tongue, or heart.

There are spaces on the pledge card for signature and date.
The card ends with this acknowledgment: "Based on the pledge drafted by Martin Luther King Jr. for the Southern Christian Leadership Conference."

The Coalition built a strong grassroots organization rapidly early in the 1990s, but its structure was severely damaged when state and county leaders resigned. The organization remains committed to rebuilding, however, and seeks volunteers to head state and county organizations. State organizations remain powerful in a few states, and the Texas chapter took the responsibility of creating and distributing all voter guides.

Under the leadership of Ralph Reed, the Christian Coalition gained the reputation as the most moderate and pragmatic of national Christian Right organizations. Reed argued that it was better to elect candidates who would deliver part of the Christian Right agenda than to hold out for ideologically pure candidates who lose to liberal Democrats. He urged the coalition's members to support Republicans such as Kay Bailey Hutchison of Texas, despite her moderate pro-choice position on abortion. Reed is also credited by some as working to soften the pro-life plank in the Republican party presidential platform, presumably to help the Republicans run on a platform that is more acceptable to the general electorate.

The Christian Coalition has a broad agenda and has devoted a good deal of energy to efforts to lobby members of Congress on behalf of conservative positions on health care, taxes, and other economic issues. Its ecumenical lobbying staff once had a solid reputation on Capitol Hill, although staff turnover has diminished its effectiveness. It is actively involved in every aspect of electoral politics, including candidate recruitment and training and especially voter mobilization.

Its most visible political activity is the distribution of voter guides in primary and general elections. The Coalition claimed to have distributed 40 million voter guides in 1998, although former staffers claim that this number was inflated (Goodstein, 1999). Nevertheless, it is clear that millions of voter guides were distributed in churches across the country.

Focus on the Family/Family Research Council

Although the Christian Coalition has received most of the media attention to the Christian Right, in 2000, the network of Focus on the Family is more active. Focus is the radio ministry of James Dobson, broadcast on more than 4,000 stations worldwide in fifteen languages. Focus employs 1,300 people and sends books, tapes, and videos to more than 9,000 people daily without charge, although there are suggested donation amounts. Dobson's broadcasts reach 5 million listeners a day, and his constituent mailing list is more than 2.5 million (Barrett, 1999). Dobson rejects the label "Christian Right," insisting instead that his organization is pro-family, although his rhetoric and agenda clearly fit within the Christian Right mainstream (Moen, 1992).

Although Focus is primarily a tax-exempt radio ministry, it is deeply involved in politics. In 1999, for example, Focus helped sponsor a large campaign to change public opinion about homosexuality and to promote the "conversion" of gays and lesbians to heterosexuality. Dobson's broadcasts are heavily political, and he meets with government officials to lobby for his preferred policies. He is also active in electoral politics, although in doing so he makes it clear that he is speaking as a private citizen, not representing Focus.

Focus has its own network of more than thirty state affiliates, which are involved in public education and lobbying efforts. State affiliates vary in their activity: some produce ratings of state legislators, others produce research reports on policy issues under debate in their state. These research reports are shared by state organizations, so a report produced in Michigan may be used by Virginia's Family Foundation to lobby state legislators, or faxed to activists in several states.

Dobson's rhetoric is uncompromising and ideological, frequently at odds with the pragmatic language of the Christian Coalition. While Ralph Reed was working to support the "big tent" conception of the GOP—the idea that the party was big enough to include supporters who disagreed on abortion—Dobson threatened to walk out the rear flap of that tent if the party abandoned its pro-life platform. "My goal is not to see the Republican Party prosper," he says, and if he leaves he said he would "do everything I can to take as many people with me as possible."

Dobson helped create the Family Research Council (FRC) in 1982, and for a time the FRC was the political arm of Focus on the Family. In 1992 the FRC split from Focus, although there remain many informal connections between the two organizations. FRC is now a tax-exempt educational organization with the following goals:

- Promote and defend traditional family values in print, broadcast, and other media outlets.
- Develop and advocate legislative and public policy initiatives that strengthen the family and promote traditional values.
- Establish and maintain an accurate source of statistical and research information that reaffirms the importance of the family in civilization.
- Inform and educate citizens on how they can promote biblical principles in culture.

For many years the head of the Family Research Council was Gary Bauer, once an aide to Education Secretary William Bennett and later domestic policy adviser in the Reagan White House. In spring 1999 Bauer took an unpaid leave from FRC to seek the GOP nomination for president. After Bauer withdrew from the campaign, he did not return to FRC, but instead worked full time to build his PAC, the Campaign for Working Families.

FRC produces policy reports that are designed to shape the policy debate, to help create a legislative agenda for Christian Right activists, and to assist movement activists in lobbying government.

Concerned Women for America

The grandmother of the contemporary Christian Right is Concerned Women for America (CWA), founded in 1979 by Beverly LaHaye. CWA today resembles in some ways the fundamentalist organizations of the 1970s, for the messages of its direct mail and newsletters are those of a moral crusade, not a political movement. Yet unlike those earlier groups, CWA has appealed beyond a narrow fundamentalist base. Moreover, unlike the rest of the early fundamentalist groups, CWA built early at the grassroots, primarily through local women's prayer and Bible groups. Indeed, it is not uncommon for the state chapter to be moribund while several local chapters are active throughout the state.

CWA moved to Washington, D.C., in 1985 and established a national office and lobbying staff, but it remains a decentralized organization. Through matching grants from major corporations, the organization has managed to maintain a focused presence in all congressional districts that enables it to use grassroots pressure as part of its lobbying strategy (Moen, 1992).

CWA once had a strong legal arm, and it provided legal assistance in many high-profile cases, including the Tennessee school textbook controversy popularly referred to as "Scopes 2" (Bates, 1993), but the group has discontinued these efforts. Its agenda is focused on matters of special concern to women, and in recent years it has added foreign policy to its concerns. CWA has been at the forefront of efforts by the Christian Right to offer a strong counter to the National Organization for Women (NOW) and other feminist groups. In many states, CWA disseminates information and voter guides, sometimes produced in coordination with state affiliates of Focus on the Family. The CWA had 1,200 local affiliates and a membership several hundred thousand strong in 1999, although precise membership estimates are not available.

The special strength of CWA is grassroots lobbying. Its members meet with national, state, and local policymakers in district offices and write letters and make phone calls to pressure policymakers. In 1999 the organization flooded Congressional phone lines with calls pressuring for an end to what is called the marriage penalty in the tax code, but GOP leaders insisted in bundling that proposal into a broad and deep tax cut that inevitably drew a presidential veto. In 2000, the House GOP leadership consented to a vote on a clean marriage-penalty bill, which passed the House with some Democratic support.

Other Organizations

Several other national organizations are active, although they lack a strong grassroots presence. The Reverend Donald Wildmon heads the **American Family Association** (AFA), formerly known as the National Federation for Decency. The AFA focuses on organizing boycotts of sponsors of television programs that contain excessive sex and violence or that the organization believes contain an anti-Christian bias. It also became involved in battles over school curricula. AFA has a radio program, a foundation, and a legal arm. Estimates of the membership of the AFA vary, and it claims 650 local chapters across the country.

The group most active in battles over public school curricula is the **Citizens for Excellence in Education** (CEE), headed by Robert Simonds. The CEE has led the fight against outcomes-based education, the Impressions reading series, and a variety of self-esteem curricula, which the group's activists frequently refer to as teaching witchcraft. It seeks to remove from the public schools texts that teach evolution and that it believes teach secular humanism. It has also been active in working to elect school board members. CEE rhetoric is confrontational: Simonds wrote in a 1994 fundraising letter, "As churches watch from the sidelines, the ungodly elect atheists and homosexuals to school boards and legislatures to enact policies and laws that destroy our Christian children and discriminate against Christian families."

One of the oldest surviving Christian Right groups is **Eagle Forum**, headed by Phyllis Schlafly [1] Founded in 1972, Eagle Forum was quite effective in fighting the proposed Equal Rights Amendment (ERA) to the U.S. Constitution. Throughout the 1970s, a majority of Americans favored the amendment, but through well-organized grassroots lobbying, Eagle Forum and other groups managed to defeat the amendment in state legislatures across the country. After that, Eagle Forum shrank in size, but it remains active in opposing efforts to add ERAs to state constitutions and in opposing legal abortion. Over the past several years, Eagle Forum has become increasingly involved in education issues. Schlafly is a long-time conservative activist who has spent much of her adult life traveling the country arguing that women should remain home with their children.

The **Traditional Values Coalition**, headed by the Reverend Louis Sheldon, has centered its activity on issues relating to gay rights, although it also takes a pro-life position on abortion and is involved in attempts to alter public school curricula. The group was involved in the Oregon and Colorado initiatives that proposed constitutional amendments to limit antidiscrimination laws against gays and lesbians, and it worked to reject a health education curriculum for California public schools that discussed issues such as homosexuality and AIDS.

The Fellow Travelers

Several organizations are best conceived as being separate from the Christian Right, although they frequently share resources with Christian Right groups and back the same candidates. Most of these groups take strongly conservative positions on political issues and link those positions in some way to religious belief. Yet most political scientists would not classify them as part of the Christian Right, for various reasons.

Foremost are the hundreds of national, state, and local pro-life groups. The National Right to Life Committee and hundreds of other pro-life groups oppose abortion rights and usually tie that position to religious belief. Yet pro-life groups are not generally identified with the Christian Right because a sizable minority of their supporters are not conservatives. In an effort to attract the widest possible audience, most pro-life groups focus their attention solely on abortion and take no official position on any other issue, including contraception, thus allowing liberals who oppose most of the Christian Right agenda to join pro-life groups.

There are substantial numbers of pro-life activists from the Catholic and evangelical Left, and the "seamless garment" network of organizations that oppose not only abortion but also the death penalty and nuclear weapons and that advocate increased spending on child welfare programs provide many members for pro-life groups.[2] Thus, although most Christian Right activists are pro-life, not all pro-life activists support the Christian Right. Yet in elections in which candidates take divergent views on abortion, the two sets of organizations often work together, and their activists frequently mingle as they volunteer on behalf of pro-life candidates.

The pro-life organization that comes closest to fitting a Christian Right label is **Operation Rescue**, which specializes in blockading abortion clinics and harassing doctors and patients. Randall Terry, the group's founder, has more explicitly linked abortion to other conservative policies. Yet studies have shown that there are liberals among the activists in Operation Rescue (Maxwell, 1994).

One large and growing segment of the public that provides substantial support to the Christian Right is homeschool advocates. Many Christian conservatives strongly object to elements of the public school curriculum, and some educate their children at home rather than send them to public schools. Like the pro-life movement, the homeschool movement tends to focus on a narrow set of issues to attract a wide diversity of membership. Moreover, there exists a small but important segment of the homeschool community that is liberal in its politics—indeed, some parents homeschool their children to prevent them from hearing nationalistic and pro-capitalist values in the classroom. Yet the homeschool constituency for the Christian Right is large and growing, and in Virginia in 1993, Michael Farris, a homeschool advocate, successfully mobilized this constituency to win the Republican nomination for lieutenant governor. Although he lost the election, Farris made plans to build a college[3] in northern Virginia to educate children who were homeschooled.

There is also significant overlap in the membership of the Christian Right and pro-gun groups. The National Rifle Association (NRA) usually has a presence at Christian Coalition meetings—as exhibitor, advertiser, or both. Especially in the South, God and guns are forces often seen moving as one.[4] Yet many Christian Right activists, especially in the North, favor gun control, and many NRA activists take libertarian positions on social issues such as abortion and homosexuality.

Secular conservative groups often work with the Christian Right to nominate the most conservative Republicans and to help them win election. They also cooperate in lobbying and have in the past provided key resources to help the Christian Right mobilize. For example, the Free Congress Foundation (FCF), headed by Paul Weyrich, is an educational and research organization. The FCF was once part of a network of organizations that included the Committee for the Survival of a Free Congress, one of the largest new Right political action committees

Randall Terry leads a New York City demonstration against easing the Republican abortion plank.

(PACs). The committee and the FCF recruited and trained candidates and campaign directors in an effort to help elect very conservative Republicans to Congress, some of whom were Christian conservatives. Today the two organizations have far less money but are still active (Gimpel, 1994).

A number of organizations combine right-wing religion and right-wing politics in ways that most Christian Right activists would find abhorrent. At the fringe of the gun community, the various militia groups that attracted attention after the Oklahoma City bombing frequently proclaim their Christian doctrine, but they are not part of the Christian Right movement, and most Christian Right activists oppose the militia groups. Many racist and anti-Semitic organizations claim a Christian grounding for their views, although their doctrine would be unpalatable to mainstream Christians. The Christian Identity Movement, for example, claims that Jews are the illegitimate spawn of Satan and that whites are the true Israelites (Barkun, 1994). The Christian Right leadership is unanimous in its condemnation of such extremist organizations.

State and Local Organizations

Although national Christian Right organizations attract most of the media atten-tion, each state has its own unique homegrown groups, and most have myriad flourishing local organizations as well. In Oregon, for example, the **Oregon Citi-zens Alliance** (OCA), originally a vehicle for a particular candidate, eventually spearheaded an effort to limit gay and lesbian rights by initiative and referenda.[5] The OCA played an important role in Republican nomination politics in the state for almost a decade and worked with the Christian Coalition and other groups to disseminate information before elections. It disbanded in 1998.

In Fairfax County, Virginia, a dispute over the distribution of the gay advocacy newspaper *The Washington Blade* at public libraries led to the formation of a countywide organization. In 1992, Karen Jo Gounaud organized a local group of Christian parents to protest the *Blade* and demand its removal from public li-braries. Her organization quickly drew advice and support from sympathetic Christian Right groups and expanded its agenda. The organization also sought to force libraries to provide parents information on the books and tapes their children had checked out and to ban a gay library employee from wearing a pink gay pride triangle on his lapel, on the grounds that it advocated a criminal lifestyle.[6]

The rapid development of this local organization headed by a previously apo-litical homemaker is testimony to the solid grassroots networking of Christian Right groups. Gounaud received training from the Christian Coalition at a 1993 political activism seminar held in Manassas, Virginia. She also received advice from the American Family Association[7] and support from key Republican county officials. She soon had a large mailing list, access to a fax network, and other trap-pings of an institutionalized organization. Her organization is hardly unique, and indeed other local Christian Right groups exist in Fairfax County. Across the country, many counties have affiliates of one or more of the three main Christian Right organizations, affiliates of one or more state-level groups, and one or more unique local organizations.

Christian Right Social Movement Organizations and Leaders: Cooperation and Conflict

The Christian Right organizations described above all share a core of common issues and complaints, but they differ subtly in their explanation of events, in their call for action, and in their issue focus. Social movement organizations and leaders often cooperate to work on a particular issue, but they also compete with one another in important ways. Movement organizations seek to mobilize the same pool of potential supporters. That pool is large but finite, and although many activists join more than one group, their average financial contribution may decrease as the number they join increases. In a real sense, Christian Right groups compete for members and money.

Perhaps more importantly, they compete for the attention of activists. Each group and leader offers a subtly different flavor of ideology, explanation, and agenda, and seeks to form the movement around that vision. The Christian Coalition argues the case for pragmatism, for supporting all GOP candidates because the party is more likely to pass legislation favorable to the movement. The Family Research Council and Focus on the Family, in contrast, both promote a more uncompromising view and argue that Republicans have taken the movement for granted because it appears to lack an effective exit strategy.

This fundamental difference carries over into legislative priorities. The Christian Coalition cautions its activists to avoid wasting resources on impossible demands such as a ban on all abortion, but instead to try to ban certain "partial-birth" abortion procedures and work for parental consent laws. Other Christian Right groups abhor compromise on abortion and call for a total ban at the earliest possible date.

The leaders of Christian Right groups also compete, and do not always cooperate. When Pat Robertson ran for president in 1988, Jerry Falwell, head of the Moral Majority, endorsed then Vice President George Bush. In 1999, when Gary Bauer sought the GOP nomination, Robertson made it clear that he backed Governor George W. Bush of Texas, and Falwell even refused to defuse a rumor linking Bauer with a sexual affair.

This competition is not unusual in social movements—it happened in the civil rights and feminist movements as well. Moreover, competition does not mean that groups do not cooperate on many issues. In the late 1980s it was not unusual to see Ralph Reed traveling the halls of Congress with James Dobson, working together on an issue.

Christian Right Groups and Their Members

Although it is possible to estimate the membership for many of the groups just discussed, it is not easy to estimate combined total membership because many of the same activists have joined several organizations. Clearly the Christian Right has formed a variety of organizations that specialize in particular tactics and in particular issues: People most concerned with secular humanism in schools join the Citizens for Excellence in Education; those who want to combat the "radical gay agenda" might join the Traditional Values Coalition; those who wish to engage in electoral mobilization can do so through the Christian Coalition; and those who wish to help prepare and disseminate research reports may choose to work for the Family Research Council.

But it is also clear that many Christian Right activists are involved in more than one group, and a core of activists have multiple involvement. Thus, the total number of activists is not as large as the sum of the membership totals of the various organizations. Political scientist John Green, who closely studies the Christian Right, estimates that there may be as many as 4 million Christian Right members nationwide and possibly 150,000 activists who do work in politics (Green, 2000). Green notes that it is possible that the total membership is significantly lower, however.

The activists themselves are generally well-educated, moderately affluent individuals who are distinctive primarily in their high levels of church attendance. They are disproportionately female, for there is a considerable talent pool of conservative Christian wives and mothers who remain out of the paid labor force for religious reasons. Many evangelical women who cannot justify taking on part-time employment find that political action is an important outlet for their energies and abilities.

Organizations communicate with their members in diverse ways. Most groups send members regular newsletters, which include information on pending legislation, the political process, activities by group leaders, and new issues being pursued. These newsletters range from poorly photocopied manuscripts prepared with simple computer software for some local groups, to glossy magazines, to electronic publications. Most groups contact their members regularly by letter, fax, and e-mail, usually asking for additional contributions in the process.

Most organizations also issue action alerts, which inform members of legislation under active consideration by some governmental body. Action alerts include explicit instructions for which officials to contact and what arguments to make. Although many action alerts still go out by mail, some groups use telephone trees, in which each activist agrees to call ten others. With the advent of home fax machines and fax modems, some groups now use fax trees, in which information faxed from the central office can quickly reach thousands of homes, and other groups send out action alerts via e-mail. There are many religious chat groups on the Internet that focus on conservative Christian concerns, and World Wide Web has home pages that provide yet another way for information to seep down to the grass roots (see Box 3.2)

Once members have been informed about issues, candidates, or events, they frequently share this information with others in their churches who may not be

. . . .

BOX 3.2

The Christian Right and Technology

Although critics often charge that Christian conservatives are opposed to any form of modernism, the movement has always used the best technology available to spread its message. In the 1920s antievolution activists used printing presses to distribute fliers, published tracts and special newspapers, and held tent revivals. In the 1950s anticommunist groups used radio to communicate with fellow travelers. In the 1980s the Moral Majority used computers to organize a direct-mail campaign to fund its organization and used television to mobilize its base.

In the 1990s the Christian Right uses technology as well as any movement in America. Its leaders continue to use radio, television, and direct mail to reach their constituents, but their efforts are more sophisticated. For example, direct-mail appeals are more carefully targeted to supporters based on their past response to solicitations, and cable television now provides programming for many market niches.

In addition, Christian conservatives use newer technologies to communicate and disseminate information. Across the country, fax chains have been organized in which each person who receives a fax transmits it to several other activists. On the Internet, most major groups now have web pages. Several are listed below. The Internet is also the home to Christian Right news groups.

Web addresses:

Christian Coalition	www.cc.org
Focus on the Family	www.family.org
Family Research Council	www.frc.org/home.html
Eagle Forum	www.eagleforum.org
American Family Association	www.afa.net
Citizens for Excellence in Education	www.nace-cee.org
Traditional Values Coalition	www.traditionalvalues.org
American Center for Law and Justice	www.aclj.org
Concerned Women for America	www.cwfa.org

These web sites are for anti-Christian Right organizations that monitor the movement:

Interfaith Alliance	www.tialliance.org
People for the American Way	www.pfaw.org
Americans United for Separation of Church and State	www.au.org

members or even necessarily supporters of the Christian Right. The frequent face-to-face interactions in churches provide an ideal opportunity to disseminate information, and in this way Christian Right arguments and issues have a much greater penetration than mere membership numbers would suggest (Wald, 1988). Individuals who would never support the Christian Coalition might nonetheless contact county school officials about the content of sex education classes or vote for a candidate whose views they shared. Moreover, many Christian conservatives receive information from a variety of Christian Right groups although they are not members and may use this information to guide their electoral behavior.

Christian Right Action in Electoral Politics

The Christian Right is active in a number of policy arenas and has pursued a variety of tactics to influence different kinds of governmental units. In general, the Christian Right has sought to influence the selection of political elites by working to help favored candidates win party nominations and then by helping them defeat their general election opponents. The movement has chosen a partisan strategy of working with the GOP, instead of attempting to influence the policies of both parties. It has also sought to influence government leaders, including those who are not supporters of the movement.

The Nomination Process

The fundamentalist groups of the 1980s and the new political organizations of the 1990s have worked to help candidates win their party's nomination. In states where nominees are selected in caucuses or statewide conventions, these groups have had considerable success. In Virginia, for example, the Moral Majority sent hundreds of delegates to Republican nominating conventions in the early 1980s, and the Christian Coalition, Family Foundation, and CWA did the same in the 1990s. In nearly all cases, the movement has been successful in helping nominate preferred candidates in Virginia. In states where nominees are selected by primary election, however, Christian Right groups have had mixed success (Green, 2000).

Christian Right involvement in nomination politics begins with candidate recruitment. Movement activists sometimes identify potential candidates from within their organizations and churches. They generally encourage a potential candidate to run for some local office and offer an array of services to help persuade the candidate to run. The Christian Coalition has provided training for candidates, their campaign managers, and their campaign finance directors. Other sympathetic conservative groups, especially the Free Congress Foundation, also provide training.

Candidate recruitment provides an invitation to struggle within the movement, for some activists prefer candidates who will take strong, uncompromising positions in support of the Christian Right agenda, whereas others prefer candidates who have a chance of winning. In general, movement leaders prefer the latter; many activists prefer the former. Thus movement leaders may recruit potential candidates who already serve in local or state office and who have demonstrated a strong record of support for Christian Right policies, but who are not themselves members of the movement. These "outsider" candidates have a greater chance of winning than those recruited from within the movement.

Of course, not all Christian Right candidates are recruited by movement leaders and activists. Evangelical religion teaches that Christians must be always listening for a call from God to perform some special service, and over the past decade, the movement has produced a number of "self starter" candidates who hear a personal call to political service. Although these individuals bring a great deal of enthusiasm to their candidacies, they generally bring little else. They lack experience in political office, in assembling electoral coalitions, and in raising money (Green, 2000). Generally they are extremely conservative and often unwilling to compromise their beliefs to win election. Self-starters therefore are prone to extreme statements or actions: When the wife of Minnesota Republican Allen Quist died while pregnant, he had the fetus removed from her body and buried in her arms.[8] The gesture may have won him the undying support of some pro-life activists, but it surely alienated him from the majority of Minnesota voters.

In recent years, the Christian Right (especially the Christian Coalition) has begun to work to discourage candidacies by movement activists, preferring instead to back more experienced politicians who would support at least some of the movement's agenda. For example, the Christian Coalition in Virginia in 1993 gave a strong early endorsement to George Allen, former congressman, for the Republican nomination for governor but did not offer early or enthusiastic assistance to Michael Farris, a former Moral Majority state director who had never held elected office, in his bid for the lieutenant governor nomination (Rozell and Wilcox, 1996).

After candidates are recruited, the movement can provide many resources for an intraparty nomination, including financial assistance, expertise, and access to a broad communication infrastructure. The most important resource, however, is voter mobilization.

Voter mobilization in intraparty nomination contests is useful in all states, but statewide nomination rules make it more valuable in some states than in others. State parties can choose to select their nominees by primary election, by convention, or by caucus, and the Christian Right has far more success in influencing nominations in states that do not use primary elections. The Christian Coalition, CWA, and the state affiliates of Focus on the Family generally put together packets of information on how and where to vote in primary elections, where and when the caucus or convention will be held, and how to register to attend. Such information is crucial in caucus and convention states where few voters participate and many citizens do not know how to go about participating in the process. It is less useful in states with primary elections, where it is relatively easy to determine when and where to vote. Included in these packets of information are profiles of various candidates, usually offered without an explicit group endorsement. But a tacit endorsement is often signaled—by the description of issue positions or even by the quality of the photos.

In states with caucuses or conventions, the Christian Right not only can be a major player in nominations but can even dominate the process, for a determined voter mobilization campaign can swamp the opposition. In Virginia's open convention system, for example, Christian Right delegates were in solid control of the nomination process in both 1993 and 1994, but in an open primary for Senate nomination in 1998 they lost badly to moderate forces. In Minnesota, Allen Quist handily defeated the popular moderate incumbent, Arne Carlson, in the state convention. But Minnesota Independent Republicans ultimately select their nominee by party primary, and Carlson defeated Quist by an overwhelming margin in that larger electoral arena.

Why is the Christian Right more influential in states with open caucuses and conventions than in states with primary elections? In most states the Christian Right represents a sizable Republican contingent but is clearly a minority. Participating in caucuses and conventions requires more effort than voting in a primary election because caucus and convention meetings sometimes last for hours or even days, and participation entails determining precisely where the local meeting will be held. In states with caucuses and conventions, the Christian Right can win because its activists are more likely to make the extra effort to participate than are party moderates. In states with primary elections, however, voting is relatively easy, and moderate voters generally outnumber supporters of the Christian Right. Thus, the ongoing nomination struggles between Christian conservatives and party moderates often hinge on the party rules that dictate how candidates are chosen.

Because these rules are set by the state party committees, the Christian Right has frequently made efforts to gain working control of state parties. In 1994,

MAP 3.1

Christian Right Influence in State Republican Parties

■ Dominant influence
▨ Substantial influence
□ Minor influence

Source: Persinos, 1994.

Campaigns & Elections reported that the Christian Right was the dominant faction in eighteen states and had substantial influence in thirteen others. At the 1995 Christian Coalition convention, Robertson announced that he would not be content until the movement extended its influence into all fifty state committees (see Map 3.1). By 2000 the overall extent of Christian Right influence had probably not changed, although there had been some change in the extent of influence in particular states.

The Christian Right is influential in state Republican parties in the South and on the West Coast and far less influential in the Northeast. In part this reflects the presence of Christian conservatives, who provide the infantry for the intraparty battle. The Christian Right has also had great success in states in transition from Democratic to Republican majorities, perhaps because they contain fewer entrenched Republican elites who resist its incursion into the party (Green, Guth, and Wilcox, 1998).

In states where the Christian Right has become an important party faction, party moderates and secular conservatives have reacted in diverse ways. Surveys of party activists have revealed that in some states, such as Minnesota and Virginia, the two factions express mutual hostility, with each preferring Democratic candidates to Republicans from the other faction of the party. In other states, such as Texas and Washington, the factional disputes are more muted. Factional battles are more likely in states where the Christian Right activist core is large but its popular support base is smaller and in states with convention systems that force activists into face-to-face confrontations (Green, 2000).

In some states, the Christian Right dominates the Republican party, and moderates complain that their party has been taken over. What does it mean to dominate a state party? In Virginia it means that the state party chair is an ally of the Christian Right and that a working majority of the state central committee is composed of activists in or sympathetic to the movement.[9] The Christian Right also controls many county Republican committees in Virginia, although moderates continue to battle movement activists. In Spotsylvania County, conservative Christians led by a local Baptist minister mobilized to oust from the county committee the GOP chair who had served for ten years and to remove moderates, including the local Republican state senator.[10] The Christian Right activists came with a plaque already prepared thanking the ousted chair for his years of service to the party. In an article in the April 30, 1994, *Richmond Times Dispatch*, Tyler Whitley commented on the struggle: "The old-line group refused to step down, describing the insurgents as 'reactionaries of the fundamentalist right,' and 'rogue elephants.' The state party, however, backs the newcomers." In Campbell County, the committee replaced the ten-year county chair with a nineteen-year-old Farris supporter, and later a group of Christian activists ousted the moderate faction from the county board as the state party chair looked on. In these county battles, the support of the state party chair was helpful to Christian Right activists. In most cases, the Christian Right forces remain in control of the party apparatus some six years later.

When Christian Right activists become the dominant force in a state party organization, they assume certain responsibilities and gain certain resources. The responsibilities include running the party on an ongoing basis, which requires time and considerable attention. In most states, however, movement activists have found the gains to be worth the investment in time and energy. First, the party has resources to help candidates, and these resources need not be divided evenly among all candidates running. The party makes direct cash contributions, has a corps of volunteers, and has connections with other interest groups that will work for and help fund candidates. Second, the party sets the rules for nominations, and control of the party means that these rules can favor insurgent groups like the Christian Right. Third, the state party writes its own platform, and this constitutes the core of the party's agenda. When Christian Right activists took control of the Washington Republican party in 1992, they wrote a platform that included opposition to the teaching of "New Age Movement Philosophy, including reincarnation, mystical powers, Satan worship, etc., as introduced in the textbooks of our education system," opposition to "mind-altering techniques for public school students," and the endorsement of parental control of textbook adoptions.[11] Few party moderates believed that the Washington state public school curriculum taught Satan worship.

Presidential Nominations

Presidential nominations are politically distinctive in many ways. They entail national campaigns that are contested state by state, they are lengthy processes that involve a rapid winnowing of the field, and they are extremely expensive. The Christian Right plays an important role in the process of presidential selection because the movement controls state party committees in many states, because some states select among the nominees by caucuses or conventions, and because the movement has ample financial resources to support a candidate.

Although movement leaders backed Ronald Reagan in the 1980 primaries and caucuses, the Christian Right was at the time a fledgling movement, and at least some who would eventually join it were still registered as Democrats in southern states. In 1984 Reagan ran unopposed, so the first real test of the strength of the Christian Right in nomination politics came in 1988 when Pat Robertson sought the presidency.

The 1988 campaign revealed that the movement had considerable resources. Although Robertson's father had been a U.S. senator and Robertson had been involved indirectly in politics for some time, he lacked experience in elected or even appointed office and was at the time an ordained minister.[12] Despite these liabilities, Robertson's campaign was surprisingly successful. He won most states with caucuses and raised more money than any previous presidential candidate.

Yet the campaign also showed some of the weaknesses of the Christian Right. Robertson lost badly in all primary elections, despite spending huge sums. Religious particularism, especially fundamentalist antipathy toward charismatics, hampered his campaign, and ultimately his support was narrowly based among pentecostal and charismatic Christians. As noted in chapter 2, he made wild statements that attracted widespread derision, and in other ways behaved like an amateur candidate.[13]

Pat Buchanan and his wife attend the 1995 Christian Coalition convention. © Mark
Peters/SABA 1995.

Robertson suffered because of his lack of experience, general public distrust of
preachers who would be president, and religious divisions among his evangelical
constituency. Yet the Christian Right can support other presidential candidates
who lack these liabilities, and in that case the Christian Right will be a formidable
force in nomination politics. The movement can provide volunteers, infrastructure, and lots of cash for favored candidates.

   In 1996 the movement was courted by several candidates with at least passable
credentials as social conservatives. Alan Keyes, Bob Dornan, and Patrick
Buchanan all had established records as social conservatives, and Phil Gramm and
Bob Dole also made strong appeals. As the campaign unfolded, movement activists divided their votes between Dole and Buchanan. Buchanan's fiery rhetoric
excited many of the movement's purists: At one rally he claimed that the founding
fathers would have had one response if they had learned that public schools did
not teach the Bible but taught about homosexuality: "Lock and load!"

   But Buchanan's candidacy came with baggage—many Christian conservatives
found evidence of racism and anti-Semitism in his speeches, and others objected
to his extreme nativism. Some fundamentalist activists may have opposed
Buchanan because of his Catholicism. More pragmatic Christian Right activists

backed Dole, whom they saw as the only candidate with a real chance to defeat President Bill Clinton.

In 2000, the field of candidates vying for Christian Right support in the primaries was large. Longtime movement activist Gary Bauer took leave from the Family Research Council to run. Senators Bob Smith of New Hampshire and Orrin Hatch of Utah sought the nomination, along with former Vice President Dan Quayle. Perennial candidates Alan Keyes and Patrick Buchanan resumed their quixotic quests. Multi-millionaire candidate Steve Forbes, who ran in 1996 as a social moderate, campaigned with the zeal of a born-again social conservative, although many movement activists questioned his sincerity.

Bauer's campaign was openly ideological, eschewing compromise on issues such as abortion. He promised:

> I will appoint men and women to the Federal judiciary who share my view of unborn children as constitutionally protected and who will unhesitatingly vote to overturn Roe v. Wade. If nominated by my party, I will select my running mate from among a list of men and women fully committed to protection of the unborn.

Yet party moderates showed their organizational muscle in the 2000 races, raising record sums of money for George W. Bush, moderate governor of Texas and son of the former president. By summer 1999 Bush had received more than 100 endorsements from House GOP members and had the support of most sitting governors as well. Many Christian conservatives complained that the "fix was in," and Smith and Buchanan eventually bolted the party, although Smith soon returned.

During the campaign, Bush appealed openly to the Christian Right and received substantial support in key states such as South Carolina. Pat Robertson's active work on behalf of Bush drew an angry rebuke from Senator John McCain. In South Carolina, Bush spoke at Bob Jones University and did not use the occasion to chasten the school for its openly anti-Catholic message nor its policies on interracial dating. Thus, ultimately it was moderate Bush who appealed most strongly to Christian conservatives and won because of their support.

When Gary Bauer dropped out of the campaign, he endorsed John McCain. McCain's subsequent attacks on Robertson, and Bauer's muted response to those attacks, left many movement activists strongly critical of Bauer. After the campaign, Bauer returned to the Campaign for Working Families, which he hoped to build into a strong national organization.

Christian Right activists have also played an active role in drafting presidential nomination platforms. Republicans select delegates to platform committees through procedures that allow organized activists a disproportionate voice, and the movement has "owned" various sections of the platform since 1980. In 1996,

Bob Dole worked hard to insert a "tolerance" plank in the platform that proclaimed that the Republican party welcomed support from those who did not
share the pro-life position of the platform. Ultimately he lost this effort. Dole
promptly announced that he had not read the platform and did not think he
would have time to do so.

General Elections

The Christian Right does not always win its intraparty struggle over nominations,
but in the November general election movement activists generally decide that
the Republican candidate is closer than the Democrat to their views and that their
policy objectives will fare better in a Congress or state legislature dominated by
Republicans.[14]

The Christian Coalition has worked hard for relatively moderate Republican
candidates, and most pragmatic activists realize the benefits that come with Republican majorities. In 1996 and again in 1998 the Christian Right supported
many vulnerable Republican incumbents in the House and Senate regardless of
their ideology in an effort to help the Republicans retain control of the U.S.
Congress.

The Christian Right focuses much of its efforts on electing Republican presidents, even moderate candidates such as George Bush and Bob Dole. These cen-
trists may not be the first choice of movement activists, but they are far more
likely to pursue conservative policies than their Democratic opponents. Clinton's
veto of a bill banning late-term abortions helped mobilize the Christian Right
against him, and its activity was generally more focused on defeating Clinton than
on electing Dole.

The Monica Lewinsky scandal in the Clinton administration, coupled with
Clinton's victories in many battles with Congress, led many movement leaders
and activists in 1999 to believe that a GOP victory in 2000 was essential to the
success of their agenda. Moreover, public support for the GOP Congress coming
out of the impeachment process was extremely low (Andolina and Wilcox, 2000).
As a consequence, Pat Robertson and other leaders worked hard in early 1999 to
make George W. Bush acceptable to Christian Right activists.

The centerpiece of Christian Right activity in the general election is voter mobilization. The Christian Coalition, CWA, and many Focus affiliates distribute
voter guides in churches and publish them in religious newspapers. The Christian
Coalition guides are supposed to be nonpartisan because of tax law, but although
they purport merely to present the positions of the two candidates, it is always
clear which candidate is preferred. In Virginia's 1994 Senate election, for example,

the Christian Coalition guide distorted the record of Democratic Senator Chuck Robb and included a very unflattering picture of him (Rozell and Wilcox, 1996).[15] Moreover, the Coalition issued two quite divergent ratings of incumbent Senator John Warner—one in the primary when he was opposed by a social conservative within the party, and another, much higher rating when he ran in the general election. In 1999, the Internal Revenue Service denied the Christian Coalition of Virginia tax-exempt status, and the organization shifted publication of the voter guides to the Christian Coalition of Texas, which had tax-exempt status.

Many pastors in conservative churches allow these voter guides to be distributed before, after, or even occasionally during services the Sunday before the election. Many pastors make a few brief remarks about the candidates at this time, and some go further. In Oklahoma, for example, U.S. Representatives Steve Largent and J. C. Watts may attend services and in some cases address the congregates, with the smiling blessing of the pastor.

These voter contact efforts are important, because many evangelicals retain a suspicion of politics and a belief that it is better to remain pure than to compromise with "the world." Although it is difficult to assess the scope of these efforts, the 1996 National Election Study revealed that 22 percent of white evangelicals were contacted by a religious group, and 19 percent saw campaign information in their place of worship. Among core evangelicals, 33 percent were contacted, and 29 percent saw campaign information in their churches. These figures are higher than for Americans in other religious traditions and are far higher than for other white Protestants. This suggests that there is substantial voter contact in white evangelical churches, mostly by Christian Right groups and activists.

The Christian Right is also a source of campaign funds for candidates. The organizations of the 1980s used political action committees to raise and distribute money, but throughout the early 1990s the new generation of groups did not form national PACs.[16] Gary Bauer's Campaign for Working Families raised more than $7 million in 1997–98 and contributed or spent more than $1 million on behalf of federal candidates, including a few Democrats. The PAC also served to help Bauer prepare for his presidential campaign, including paying for consultants and helping him refine his direct-mail solicitation lists. Other Christian Right groups have national PACs, including the Eagle Forum, and the Christian Coalition currently plans to form a PAC in response to the IRS ruling against it. There are also state organizations that raise and distribute funds. Michael Farris's Madison Project, for example, contributes money early to state legislative candidates who support the Christian Right agenda.

More important, activists can help raise money for candidates, and candidates for the Senate or the presidency can mail to lists of Christian Right contributors asking for funds. Activists have shown a great willingness to give to candidates who espouse their cause. Many are willing to volunteer their time as well as money, providing candidates backed by the Christian Right with what has been called an "army that meets on Sunday."

School Board Elections

States may dictate that local school board members are appointed or elected, or states may leave these decisions to counties or other local government units. The Christian Right has in recent years made a major effort to increase the number of states and counties that elect school boards and to encourage conservative Christians to seek election to these boards. School board elections are usually low-information contests: Few citizens bother to vote, and those who do typically can recognize only a few names on the ballot. This makes it possible for a well-organized minority to have great success in such elections.

   Yet in many of these elections, the Christian Right faces well-organized, well-funded opposition from national teachers unions and groups of progressive parents who oppose the Christian Right agenda for public schools. Whenever officials of the National Education Association (NEA) or other teachers group recognize an attempt by the Christian Right to control a school board, they frequently mobilize supporters in opposition. In many high-profile elections, Christian Right slates have been defeated, including in Virginia Beach, Virginia, home of Pat Robertson's business empire. It is therefore advantageous for Christian Right candidates to avoid recognition by opposition groups, and stealth candidacies persist in school board elections in some areas.

   In 1993 the Christian Coalition led a move by conservative Christians to oust Joseph Fernandez, the chancellor of the New York City public schools, and to end a multicultural "rainbow curriculum" that included such controversial books as *Heather Has Two Mommies*, a story about a girl raised by lesbian parents. The Christian Coalition and other groups helped to assemble slates of conservative Christian candidates for many of the city's thirty-two school districts. The coalition prepared 550,000 voter guides for distribution in 1,300 white evangelical, Catholic, and black churches (Reed, 1994a). The Christian conservative slates won about as often as those backed by the liberals, and the curriculum was revised under the directorship of a new school board leader. (Dillon, 1993a; 1993b; Randolph, 1993).

   In one recent study of Christian Right school board candidacies, Melissa Deckman (1999) found that although there have been many candidacies by conservative Christians for school boards, few candidates reported that they had been recruited by Christian Right groups. Instead, many were motivated by their religious beliefs and concerns over curricular matters—concerns perhaps intensified by information provided by Christian Right groups.

Although Christian Right candidacies are increasing rapidly in school board races, Christian conservative majorities in school boards are rare across the country. In many districts, Christian conservatives hold one or two seats, however, and in some other districts a single seat could create a majority for the Christian Right. But where Christian conservatives have won a majority, voters have frequently turned them out of office in the next election. In Vista, California, for example, petitioners succeeded in winning a special election in 1994 in which Christian conservative members of the school board were defeated by moderate and liberal candidates (Jacobs, 1995).

In 1999, however, a state school board in Kansas with a Christian Right majority announced that the recommended state curriculum would no longer include core teachings of biology, astronomy, and geology that are inconsistent with Creationism. The Kansas action left counties free to teach evolution, but removed it from state science tests. The Kansas decision was one of a string of policy shifts in several states to deemphasize the teaching of evolution.

The Christian Right As Target: Countermobilization

Although the Christian Right has impressive abilities to mobilize on behalf of candidates in nomination contests and general elections, it also serves as a potent symbol against which to rally secularists, liberals, and even religious moderates. In Virginia in 1994, Christian Right activists won the GOP Senate nomination for Oliver North, only to see him lose despite a nationwide GOP landslide. In Washington state Christian Right activists helped Linda Smith win the party primary for a Senate bid in 1998, but she ultimately lost in the general election because many voters saw her as too closely tied to the Christian Right. In California in 1997, Christian conservatives spent time and money helping a socially conservative legislator beat a more moderate candidate in a special primary House election, only to see that candidate lose in a general election that many observers believe the more moderate Republican could have won. In many states, candidates who run with close ties to the Christian Right have lost when those who oppose its agenda have mobilized to defeat them.

Democratic candidates often attempt to paint Republican candidates as tools of the Christian Right. When that effort succeeds, the candidates usually lose. The Christian Right has dealt with this problem in several ways. For a time, some Christian Right candidates sought to deflect this countermobilization by hiding their ties to the movement. More recently, movement leaders have encouraged candidates to run on a broad array of issues and to speak the secular language of politics at most campaign events. Overall, however, the backing of the Christian Right is a mixed blessing. Candidates do best when they win the support of the Christian Right without being perceived as part of the movement. A candidate who can successfully appeal to the Christian conservatives without appearing to most voters to be a Christian Right activist can benefit from the quiet voter mobilization by the Christian Coalition and other organizations without prompting a countermobilization of moderates and liberals. When voters believe that a candidate is part of the Christian Right, however, countermobilization efforts are frequently (though not always) successful.

Initiatives and Referenda

The Christian Right has also been active in promoting state and local initiatives and referenda, usually on matters dealing with homosexuality. In some cases, these efforts have sought to amend state constitutions (Reed, 1998) in ways that might permanently disadvantage gays and lesbians in the political process.

In Colorado, Christian Right activists promoted a successful statewide initiative to overturn all city laws banning discrimination against gays and lesbians and to prohibit the state from ever adopting such laws in the future. The U.S. Supreme Court overturned the Colorado measure by a 6–3 vote in May 1996, primarily because it would have permanently barred a group from future political victories.

Oregon's Citizens Alliance placed a more radical initiative on the state ballot in 1992, which was narrowly defeated. It would have included language in the state constitution labeling homosexuality "abnormal, wrong, unnatural, and perverse" and it would have required public schools to teach children that homosexuality should be avoided. The year after the defeat of the initiative, thirteen cities and counties in Oregon voted to prohibit antidiscrimination legislation in their local jurisdictions (Gamble, 1995).

Although the leaders of Oregon's Citizens Alliance promised to work to place similar initiatives on the ballot in a number of states in 1994, ultimately they were unsuccessful. In many states political elites maneuvered to keep these issues off the ballot, and in other states the petition drives simply failed to attain the requisite number of signatures.

In Maine a group called **Concerned Maine Families** succeeded in 1995 in gaining ballot access for a referendum that would have prevented the state or any locality from passing legislation to ban discrimination against homosexuals. A

••

BOX 3.3

A New Breed of Candidate

In recent years, a new breed of Christian conservative candidate has appeared. Unlike movement activists or self-starters, these new candidates often have considerable political experience. Unlike "bilingual" candidates who merely appeal to Christian conservatives, they have explicit ties to the movement. But many have support from other groups as well, having assembled sophisticated political coalitions like any successful candidate.

Virginia's Attorney General Mark Early is a perfect example of this type of candidate. Early has clear ties to the Christian Right, but he has substantial political experience that prevents his Democratic (and GOP primary) opponents from characterizing him as an extremist. He served in the state Senate for ten years and had a strong reputation for effectiveness. In addition, Early has support from labor and the civil rights community—both traditional Democratic constituency groups. This support helps Early mightily in general election campaigns, and it also serves as evidence that he is not an ideologue.

Early may well be the state's next governor. In the past, movement activists such as Mike Farris and Oliver North have lost badly in Virginia, in part because Democrats successfully mobilized moderates against them. Pragmatic candidates such as George Allen and James Gilmore have appealed to Christian conservatives, but have adopted different rhetoric in different circumstances. Early is a movement candidate with considerable political skills and a broad coalition. This is the type of candidate most likely to succeed in American politics. (Rozell and Wilcox, 2000).

---

similar bill had passed the Maine legislature in 1993 but was vetoed by the governor. Other statewide organizations formed to join the campaign, and Focus on the Family provided some assistance (Hale, 1995). Ultimately the referendum was defeated 53 percent to 47 percent.

The movement has worked to pass or oppose initiatives and referenda in other policy areas as well, including abortion, state equal rights amendments for women, and gambling. In 1999, the Christian Right combined with moderate churches and liberals to defeat a lottery proposal in Alabama that would have generated revenues for schools. [17]

Lobbying Government

Although much of the focus of the contemporary Christian Right has been electoral, these organizations lobby government using the same techniques and tools as other organizations. They approach members of the national executive, legislative, and judicial branches in different ways seeking to advance their policies. The Christian Right is especially active in lobbying state and local governments.

The Presidency

In every presidential election since 1980, the Christian Right has concentrated its efforts on electing the Republican candidate. There are several reasons for this focus. First, the president has ready access to national media and so is ideally located to participate in a moral crusade. The "bully pulpit" is an important resource in efforts to persuade the public of particular goals. America's civil religion seems to require that the president assume the role of national religious leader, and if that were to entail assuming a prophetic stance on behalf of a conservative agenda, the Christian Right would surely benefit. Second, the president controls many key appointments in the bureaucracy and therefore has substantial influence on the way the bureaucracy makes new rules and interprets laws. Third, the president selects the men and women who fill the nation's judiciary and therefore indirectly shapes the types of decisions made by the courts. Finally, for most of the 1980s, it appeared unlikely that the Republicans could ever capture control of Congress, so the presidency was the only realistic national electoral goal. The movement has had one president who was rhetorically sympathetic to the movement, and it attempted to lobby and influence his administration in several ways.

In 1980 the Christian Right celebrated the election of Ronald Reagan. Although Reagan was the only divorced man ever to win the White House and seldom attended church services, he ran as a pro-family candidate and openly courted the support of conservative evangelicals. Although he had once, as governor of California, signed the most liberal abortion law in the nation, Reagan ran as a pro-life candidate in 1980, and his supporters promised privately that he would appoint only pro-life judges to the Supreme Court. Reagan supported the elimination of a long-time GOP platform plank endorsing the ERA and the insertion of a pro-life plank.

Reagan appointed Christian Right activists and supporters to visible posts in his administration. A Moral Majority leader, Bob Billings, assumed a post in the Department of Education, and antiabortion activist C. Everett Koop became surgeon general. James Watt, Reagan's choice to head the Department of Interior, reportedly argued that the imminent second coming of Christ meant that there was little need to preserve the environment.[18] Gary Bauer, who later became head of the Family Research Council and a presidential candidate, served in Reagan's second term as the head of his domestic policy team.

Reagan (and later his successor, George Bush) also ordered the bureaucracy to interpret laws in ways that pleased Christian Right activists. Perhaps the most famous example was the "gag rule" on abortion, which barred the disbursement of public funds to any family planning organization that discussed abortion with its patients. Moreover, Reagan provided many symbolic benefits to conservative Christians: He addressed pro-life rallies in Washington via White House intercom and mentioned Christian Right issues in his televised speeches.[19]

Yet ultimately many Christian Right activists became disenchanted with the Reagan administration. They argued that Christian conservatives received primarily symbolic gestures, while Reagan concentrated the energies of his administration on satisfying economic conservatives, by providing sharp tax cuts for corporations and affluent Americans, and on satisfying foreign policy conservatives through a massive military buildup. Reagan's first Supreme Court appointment was Sandra Day O'Connor, who did not vote to overturn *Roe v. Wade*, and his administration did not work to help pass a constitutional amendment that would have allowed prayer in public schools, despite heavy lobbying by the Moral Majority.

This disenchantment grew during the Bush administration, as key Christian conservatives criticized the president's moderation on social issues, exemplified by his inclusion of openly gay activists at the ceremonial signing of the Hate Crimes Act.

Michael Farris blasted both the Reagan and Bush administrations for giving nothing more to Christian conservatives than "a bunch of political trinkets." He argued that the Republican presidents provided "very little real progress in terms of advancing our public policy goals or getting our kind of people appointed to positions of real influence."[20] His views represent those of many Christian conservatives.

The election of Bill Clinton, however, focused attention on the contrast between candidates of the two parties. Within weeks of his election, Clinton signed executive orders lifting restrictions on abortion rights and appointed feminists to key administration posts. More important, the first major struggle for his administration was over the president's effort to lift the ban on open military service by gays and lesbians. Clinton quickly became the focus of intense Christian Right attacks and a very successful fundraising foil. Suddenly the Bush presidency seemed like the good old days, and the movement became focused on electing a GOP president. In 1996 the movement worked hard for Bob Dole, and some leaders such as Ralph Reed argued that the GOP must nominate Dole instead of Buchanan (whose views were more compatible with most movement activists) because Dole was more electable.

Soon after Clinton began his second term, the story broke of his affair with a White House intern. Clinton initially denied the story publicly and under oath, but eventually was forced to admit the matter when Lewinsky produced physical evidence. Christian Right activists and supporters were outraged by what they saw as public immorality by a figure who is supposed to play a key role in American civil religion. Many sermons compared Clinton to immoral kings in the Old Testament, and Christian Right leaders pushed hard on Congress to impeach and remove the president.

Yet the general public did not abandon Clinton, choosing to frame his behavior as personal, not professional. Indeed, popular support for Clinton reached its apex during his trial in the Senate (Andolina and Wilcox, 2000). Eventually Robertson backed away from the impeachment effort, leading many Christian Coalition leaders to complain that the organization had urged them to push hard for impeachment, and then not given them any warning of the retreat from that position.

Christian Right leaders assigned electing a GOP president in 2000 as their top priority, and they anticipate that a Republican president who works with a Republican Congress would pass significant portions of their issue agenda.

Congress

The president is the most visible figure in American politics, but Congress drafts and passes legislation, passes the budget, and approves treaties and appointments. No matter how enthusiastically a president may support a bill backed by the Christian Right, there are real limits on his ability to steer it through the legislature. Christian Right groups have fielded full-time congressional lobbyists since 1980, but they have had only limited success.

Until 1995, Christian Right lobbyists faced a Democratic majority in the House of Representatives, and Democrats controlled the U.S. Senate between 1987 and 1995. Democratic party leaders were not receptive to Christian Right policies, but even the Republican-controlled Senate in the early 1980s defeated a proposed constitutional amendment to allow prayer in public schools and failed to pass the tuition tax credit that Christian Right activists sought.

During the 1980s, Christian Right lobbying was generally unsophisticated and frequently alienated even supporters of the movement's policy goals. This was especially true of the Moral Majority, which succeeded in angering even Republican

Senator Orrin Hatch, a conservative Mormon sympathetic to the organization's objectives (Moen, 1989). Once important legislation such as the Equal Access Act was under consideration, Moral Majority activists did not participate in the bargaining as the legislation was being rewritten, and their public comments were widely seen by even their allies as harmful (Hertzke, 1988).

The strength of the Christian Right in the 1980s was clearly grassroots, outsider mobilization. The Moral Majority frequently mobilized its members to bury Congress in mail and phone calls. Often these appeals were misleading. While Congress was considering legislation to reverse Supreme Court decisions on civil rights, Falwell mobilized his followers by telling them that the bill would classify sin as a handicap and then force churches to hire as youth counselors "active homosexuals, transvestites, alcoholics, and drug addicts, among others" (O'Hara, 1989, p. 13).

In the 1990s the Christian Coalition, Focus on the Family and Family Research Council proved far more sophisticated than the Moral Majority in their lobbying efforts. All three organizations, along with CWA, have become skilled not only at grassroots pressure but also at the subtle art of the inside strategy—contacting and persuading congressional members. The Christian Coalition employed an ecumenical staff of professional lobbyists who established a reputation for providing accurate information, playing by the rules, and building effective if sometimes unusual coalitions. The FRC has specialized in providing detailed policy analysis to staffers and sympathetic members.

Concerned Women for America built a special network for more sophisticated grassroots lobbying. Its "535 Program" focused on developing a core of women to track legislation and the voting intentions of members of Congress. The women would communicate this information to women in each congressional district, in turn they would contact the member's home office, organize prayer chains, and otherwise focus pressure on the member if needed (Hertzke, 1988; Moen, 1992).

When the new Republican majority took office in the House and Senate in January 1995, Christian Right lobbyists suddenly had access to the majority party. A significant portion of the new GOP majority were active evangelical Christians (Guth and Kellstedt, 1999). Moreover, because many observers credited the Christian Right with increasing turnout among white evangelicals and thereby helping elect many Republicans in close contests, Republican leaders openly promised a "payback time" to vote on items from the Christian Right agenda. House Speaker Newt Gingrich promised a vote on a school prayer amendment by July 1995, but he did not deliver on that promise. The first months of the legislative session were taken up with passing the Contract with America and dealing with budget issues, and the Christian Coalition played an active role in helping promote the Contract, waiting patiently until after the House had dealt with these matters before pursuing congressional action on its agenda.

By spring 2000, however, the GOP Congress had given the Christian Right few policy victories. The Defense of Marriage Act was an important symbolic victory for the movement, allowing states to refuse to honor marriages between two gay men or lesbians performed in another state. To date no state has allowed gays or lesbians to marry, but in 2000 Vermont established domestic partnerships that conveyed many of marriage's legal benefits.(Lewis and Edelson, 2000). A ban on Internet pornography was incorporated in a telecommunications bill, but the Supreme Court overturned this provision in 1997. Tax cuts for families with children and an end to the "marriage penalty" passed the House and Senate in 1999, but party leaders ultimately chose not to submit the bill to Clinton, hoping instead to use the issue for electoral advantage. Finally, the House and Senate both passed a bill banning one late-term abortion procedure, but Clinton vetoed the measure because it did not allow for an exception to protect the health of the mother, and Congress failed to override the veto.

Many activists were openly critical of the GOP Congress for its failure to deliver on promises to movement leaders. Patrick Buchanan left the party in fall 1999, charging that there were no real differences between the Republicans and Democrats. Other activists remained hopeful that the GOP Congress would respond to the active leadership of a Republican president.

The Courts

Although Christian Right activists have focused much of their attention on electing presidents and members of Congress, U.S. Supreme Court rulings most frequently are the focus of their anger. The 1962 decision *Engel v. Vitale*, in which the court ruled that daily classroom prayer violated the establishment clause of the First Amendment, and the 1973 *Roe v. Wade* ruling that overturned state laws banning abortion convinced Christian conservatives that they needed to work to change the composition of the U.S. Supreme Court. After Reagan appointed many new justices, however, the court still upheld the basic abortion right in *Webster v. Reproductive Health Services* in 1989, and after George Bush appointed still other new justices the court struck down a "voluntary" prayer at a high school graduation ceremony in *Lee v. Weisman* in 1992.

As a consequence, many Christian conservatives continue to perceive the Rehnquist Court as a liberal institution. In the 1996 NES data, core evangelicals clearly perceived the Court as liberal, whereas other Americans saw the Court as neither liberal nor conservative.[21]

Although Christian Right leaders and activists often refer to the Rehnquist court as liberal and antireligious, in recent years they have formed special organizations designed to change public policy through litigation. Pat Robertson formed the **American Center for Law and Justice** (ACLJ) in 1990, and he promotes the group as the Christian counterpart to the American Civil Liberties Union (ACLU). The ACLJ is especially active in cases involving church-state issues. The American Family Association Law Center, founded by the Reverend Donald Wildmon in 1990, has been active in cases defending state and local obscenity and sodomy laws and Operation Rescue protesters. The Concerned Women for America also has a small unit that litigates. Michael Farris heads the **Home School Legal Defense Association,** where he devotes much of his time to defending the rights of homeschooling parents nationwide. In recent years the number of Christian Right legal groups has grown, and all groups have become more active. There are many other conservative legal groups, such as the Rutherford Institute, which take cases of interest to the Christian Right.

In recent years these groups have frequently engaged in litigation against public school boards. Some cases involve students who were allegedly prevented by school officials from reading their Bibles or praying; others involve public school curricula.[22] Attorneys for these groups frequently argue that their clients have endured discrimination because of their religious beliefs or that their right to free exercise of religion has been denied. In many cases the threat of a lawsuit is sufficient to change school board policy; in others the threat of suit by the Christian Right balances that by the ACLU, and the counterthreats enable board members to vote their own religious preferences.

The ACLJ has sponsored since 1991 an annual "See You at the Pole" day on which students gather around their high school flagpole for a student-led prayer. The ACLJ claims that millions of students now participate in these events.

The Rutherford Institute provided free legal counsel for Paula Jones in her sexual harassment lawsuit against President Clinton. Although a federal judge dismissed the Jones lawsuit, material from the discovery portion of the case eventually led to the Lewinsky scandal and impeachment. The Rutherford Institute does not as a rule provide free counsel for sexual harassment cases, and most observers believe that the group did so in this case because of the potential political damage to President Clinton.

State and Local Governments

Today Christian Right groups focus much of their attention and energy on state and local governments because many of the issues of greatest concern to the

Christian Right are decided at those levels. State and local governments decide what kinds of regulations to impose on Christian schools, what kinds of books to assign in public schools, and whether and how to teach about human sexuality. State governments can impose some kinds of restrictions on abortion access, including banning abortions in public hospitals, insisting that teenage girls obtain parental consent before having an abortion, and requiring doctors to inform the women about the development of the fetus and about the alternative of adoption.

In many states, Christian Right organizations employ lobbyists and mobilize grassroots pressure on governors, state attorneys general, members of the state legislature, and on local government officials. The kinds of policies Christian conservatives seek from state and local governments vary somewhat in different states, but Virginia provides a useful illustration. Governor George Allen won in Virginia in 1993 with the strong support of the Christian Coalition, the Family Foundation, and the CWA. During his term, he appointed Christian Right activists to key positions. His director of constituent services was a former lobbyist for the Family Foundation, his secretary of administration was a former executive director of the Virginia Society for Human Life, his secretary of health and human services was a former public affairs director of the National Right to Life Committee, and his director of personnel and training was former director of the Family Foundation. The state secretary of education was a visible opponent of the Family Life Education (FLE) program and an advocate of private-school vouchers, and the superintendent of public instruction, William C. Bosher Jr., was an advocate of student-initiated prayer and opposed requirements that school districts offer a sex education curriculum.

Allen's policy proposals also demonstrated his commitment to his Christian Right constituency. He pushed for parental notification on abortion and for student-initiated prayer. He proposed eliminating state regulation of sex education and requiring that parents actively request that their child receive sex education, replacing a system that allowed parents to opt their child out of the program. He appointed a commission on champion schools, which would have allowed religious schools to compete for state funds.

In 1995 the governor submitted new guidelines for statewide social studies teaching standards for kindergarten through twelfth grade. His appointees to the state department of education pushed for a number of initiatives popular with Christian conservatives, including the teaching of Bible stories and, for the English curriculum, the use of phonics to teach reading. When teachers statewide vigorously objected to the Allen guidelines, the department withdrew the initiative.[23]

A Christian conservative favorite, Virginia Gov. George Allen, speaks at the 1994 Republican Governors Conference. © Shepard Sherbvell/SABA 1994.

Ultimately Allen did not succeed in implementing many policies that appealed to the Chrstian Right, but his rhetorical support and his appointments sent a clear signal that he supported many of their policies. Allen faced a Democratic legislature for much of his term; many observers believe that incumbent Attorney General Mark Early will serve as the state's next governor. Early has strong ties to the Christian Right and would serve with a GOP-controlled state legislature.

From county government the Christian Right often seeks policies relating to schools and libraries. In many counties, Christian Right groups push for "adults only" sections in public libraries that would include all books to which they object, in others they seek to remove books and magazines, and in others they seek to force the library boards to buy materials published by Christian Right organizations. In a few counties, Christian Right activists have sought to end after-school child care in the public schools, arguing that such policies make it easier for women to work outside the home.

Conclusion

The Christian Right is composed of a set of national, state, and local social movement organizations that compete and cooperate in political action. These groups
vary in their issue agenda and tactics and attract different sets of activists. Overall,
the movement employs a wide variety of tactics to influence elections and public
policy.

The diversity and growing power of the Christian Right are a source of great
solace to its supporters but of great concern to those who oppose its agenda. It is
precisely because of the growing effectiveness of the Christian Right that the
movement generates such controversy. Different conceptions of the Christian
Right are explored in the next chapter.

4

··

Assessing the
Christian Right

If religious conservatives took their proper,
proportionate place as leaders in the political and
cultural life of the country, we would work to create the
kind of society in which presumably all of us would like
to live: safe neighborhoods, strong families, schools that
work, a smaller government, lower taxes. Civil rights
protections would be afforded to all Americans.

—Ralph Reed, *Politically Incorrect*, p. 10

At its core, the Christian Coalition seeks an agenda that
threatens liberty. Behind their mild rhetoric lurks an
undeniable truth: Coalition leaders want to create a
Christianized government that criminalizes abortion,
denies gays and lesbians basic rights of citizenship, and
dictates when and how public school children should
pray.

—People for the American Way,
The Two Faces of the Christian Coalition, p. 2

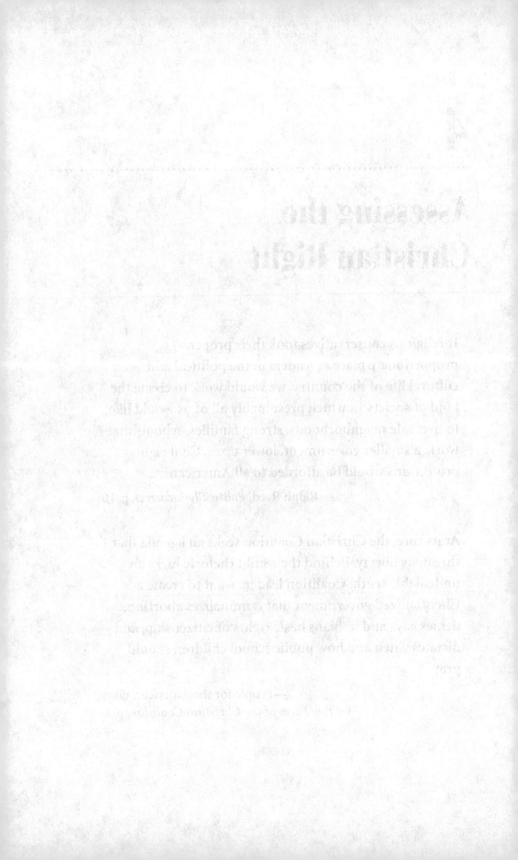

$\mathbf{T}$HE CHRISTIAN RIGHT IS A DEEPLY CONTROVERSIAL element of American politics. Its activists depict a movement that seeks to defend the rights of conservative Christians to freely exercise their religious beliefs, whereas its opponents describe a movement of moral censors who would impose their interpretation of biblical law on all Americans. At their most extreme, these divergent views of the Christian Right paint a picture of stalwart Christians battling satanic forces for the soul of America or of neo-Nazi storm troopers rounding up homosexuals or roasting marshmallows in the flames from the books they have culled from the public library.

Christian Right direct-mail publications sometimes allege that Christians are in imminent danger of being forbidden to carry Bibles to work, to wear a religious lapel pin or necklace, or even to worship on Sunday. Despite this extreme rhetoric, there is no real controversy about the right of religious conservatives to worship or to mobilize their beliefs into political action. No one is proposing that preachers be forbidden from talking about politics, or that Christians be prosecuted and fed to the hungry lions at the National Zoo.

Instead, at the heart of this dispute is whether Christian Right involvement in politics is good or bad for America. The question posed by opponents of the movement is whether the Christian Right is a dangerous force that might eventually undermine constitutional freedoms in an effort to impose its interpretation of biblical law on the United States. The question posed by Christian conservatives is whether government and society are so biased against religious faith that Christians must band together to protect their way of life.

This chapter examines the dilemma of the Christian Right. The first section explores the question of whether support for the Christian Right is rational. Many scholars from the 1950s argued that supporters exhibited pathological personalities or were deeply alienated from society, but more recent scholarship has rejected that view. The next section poses two important questions: Does the Christian Right promote democratic participation, and does it promote democratic values?

The final section considers the policies the Christian Right really seeks to implement, using proclamations by movement elites, data from surveys and in-depth interviews with movement activists. The section includes a discussion of the disagreements among Christian Right leaders and activists on precisely what policies to pursue in each area and an analysis of what the public thinks of those policy proposals.

Is the Christian Right "Rational"?

When sociologists who studied the Right in the 1950s and 1960s wrote about the movement, they used terms such as "paranoid style," "authoritarian," and "dogmatic." These scholars were generally not focusing on the Christian Right of that period but rather on the more secular organizations, such as the John Birch Society, but they undoubtedly would have used the same terms to describe the Christian Anti-Communism Crusade.[1] Scholars argued that support for the Right in the 1950s came largely from individuals who had personality disorders, who had anxiety about their social status, or who were alienated from society.[2]

It is not surprising that scholars of the 1950s feared the Right and sought to portray its supporters as irrational. The world was still coming to terms with the frightening legacy of the German Nazi party and seeking to explain how Germany—with its vibrant cultural life and basic democratic institutions—was within a decade transformed from the Weimar Republic into a nation that committed atrocities against Jews, homosexuals, and gypsies. The Nazis began by imposing seemingly minor restrictions on Jews and gradually escalated into genocide. Many feared that a similar dynamic might be possible in the United States.

Moreover, the Right of the 1950s seemed irrational, and its leaders embraced strange conspiracy theories. Great prominence was given, for example, to the role of the Illuminati, a seventeenth-century European Masonic group, in guiding a worldwide conspiracy of Jews, communists, and world bankers. The unlikely collaboration of world bankers and communists is perhaps symptomatic of the bizarre networks envisioned by the 1950s Right.[3]

The explanations for support for the Right offered by sociologists and political scientists of the 1950s focused on social and psychological pathologies that were thought to have led to support for the German Nazi party and for the American Right. Two of these explanations are considered here with respect to the contemporary Christian Right: that support for the movement comes from individuals who have troubled personalities or who are alienated from society. If true, these explanations would have some important implications for any assessment of dangers posed by the Christian Right.

Personality Explanations

A number of social psychologists in the 1960s wrote that support for the Right (and sometimes for the extreme Left) came from individuals with distinctive, distorted personalities. The most prominent charge was that supporters of the Right had authoritarian personalities. In a massive tome published in 1950, several psychologists described the authoritarian personality as involving displacement of self-hatred into aggression toward out-groups and support for right-wing figures.[4] The logic of the argument implies that individuals with authoritarian personalities should have hatred for certain out-groups such as gays, lesbians, and feminists and reverence for strong right-wing leaders such as Pat Robertson or Rush Limbaugh, the radio commentator. Subsequent writers have attributed other personality disorders, especially dogmatism and the inability to tolerate ambiguity, to supporters of the Christian Right.

Why would the Christian Right appeal to such individuals? Those who argue for a personality link suggest that the Christian Right encourages hatred for feminists, gays and lesbians, and other liberal groups and provides a vehicle for its supporters to enhance their self-worth by fighting against these insidious forces. Indeed, surveys do show that many Christian Right activists view these groups as almost satanic and see their crusade as rescuing America from evil.[5]

In addition, the Christian Right offers a straightforward portrait of a struggle between the forces of darkness and light, symbolism that has strong appeal to those who cannot tolerate ambiguity. Such accounts resonate with biblical allusions to the struggle between God and Satan and invite their adherents to conceive of conspiracies to explain the apparent collusion among forces opposed to the movement. Finally, authoritative pronouncements from ministers who interpret the inerrant word of God enable the Christian Right to offer strong leaders who are especially appealing to those with authoritarian personalities.

If personality explanations for support of the Christian Right are true, then the movement might be truly dangerous, full of maladjusted activists ready to follow whatever suggestions they receive from their leaders. Descriptions of recent assassins of abortion providers suggest that there are indeed some individuals at the fringe of the Christian Right and pro-life movements who may exhibit disturbed personalities of a dangerous sort. Other, less frightening disordered personalities doubtless exist. When I asked one Moral Majority county chair why he was involved in the movement, he told me in a serious voice that he was worried about "rampant bestiality" in the high schools. His account revealed more about his personality than about the behavior of the adolescent boys in this rural farming community.

All movements, however, attract on their fringe individuals with disordered lives. Anyone who has interviewed activists in almost any political movement can point to a few whose personalities fit these theories—and this holds true for liberal groups such as environmentalists and feminists. The real question is whether the Christian Right has any *special* appeal to such personalities and whether they constitute a sizable number of movement adherents.

One survey of Moral Majority activists in Indiana showed that a sizable minority exhibited signs of authoritarianism and feelings of inadequacy (see Table 4.1). A majority felt that strong leaders would be preferable to laws and talk, and more than a third found it inexcusable to disobey an order. Nearly a third felt guilty when they questioned authority, and another 22 percent felt no guilt because they reported they never questioned authority. There was evidence of feelings of personal inadequacy as well. The data show that those individuals with the strongest evidence of authoritarianism were the least active in the Moral Majority, which suggests that the organization succeeded in keeping maladjusted members at the margins (Wilcox, Jelen, and Linzey, 1995).

These results are difficult to interpret without a comparison with the public or with activists in other organizations, and it is likely that some Americans who oppose the Christian Right would give similar responses. Yet the data do suggest that the Christian Right attracts some individuals whose personalities resemble those posited by the social theorists of the 1950s.

Available evidence also suggests that whatever the Christian Right position on groups regarded as sinful or as political enemies, the attitudes are not generally anti-Semitic or racist. Supporters of the Christian Right are not cooler toward Jews or blacks than other white Americans. In fact, one study indicated that Christian Right activists in the Virginia Republican party were actually warmer toward Jews and blacks than were other Republicans.[6]

A number of studies suggest that Christian Right activists show no evidence of having disproportionate personality problems (Wilcox, 1992), but none of the data is definitive. My judgment, based on in-depth interviews with activists in the Christian Right, environmentalist, feminist, and other movements is that most Christian Right activists are as well adjusted as most activists in other movements. At minimum, it is fair to say that a majority of Christian Right activists show no evidence of personality disorders.

What is striking about Christian Right activists, however, is the extent of their fear of their political opponents. The rhetoric of many Christian Right leaders, especially in fundraising appeals, portrays a coalition of liberals, feminists, gays and lesbians, and others bent on destroying America and on limiting religious freedom for Christians. Although the feminist, environmental, and civil rights ac-

....

TABLE 4.1

Personality Traits Among Indiana Moral Majority Activists
(percent of respondents, N = 162)

Authoritarianism	
Strong leaders are better than laws and talk	58
Disobeying orders is inexcusable	38
Obedience is the most important virtue in children	75
I feel guilty when I question authority	27
I sometimes question authority	78
Feelings of inadequacy	
I do not have much to be proud of	12
I take a positive attitude toward myself	39
I wish I respected myself more	21
Alienation	
I am alienated or on the fringe of society	40
I never feel useless since joining the Moral Majority	39
Membership in the Moral Majority makes me feel worthy	43

Source: Survey data provided by Sharon Georgianna Linzey.

tivists I have interviewed dislike their political opponents, Christian Right activists are far more likely to truly despise them.[7] The vehemence of some movement members can be quite strong, especially in their hatred of gays and lesbians. In Fairfax County, Virginia, liberals who testified at library board meetings in favor of allowing distribution of a gay newspaper reported being pushed, shoved, and spat at, and some received death threats (Rozell and Wilcox, 1996). Coupled with the repeated death threats against abortion providers in the United States and the killings of several doctors, it is clear that the fringe of the Christian Right and related organizations includes some dangerous citizens.

Of course, pushing, shoving, and even death threats are not unique to the Christian Right. Indeed, Christian Right activists in Maine organizing a referendum against gay rights reported receiving death threats. There is no evidence that the Christian Right is especially prone to violence; rather, political groups of all types that engage in direct action over emotional issues attract some activists who cross the line of acceptable behavior. And violence is more likely if an activist fears or despises those on the other side—emotions more common among Christian Right activists.

Alienation

A second, related explanation offered by sociologists for support for the Christian Right has been that mass society has produced a substantial number of isolated individuals who lack attachments to extended families or to social institutions or groups. These rootless individuals are thought to be attracted to organizations that have strong leaders and provide the opportunity to interact and form ties with like-minded citizens. Conover and Gray argued that such individuals are easily mobilized by political groups: "Without such organizational involvement in their lives, people are thought to grow restless and alienated. . . . such individuals are 'easy prey' for right-wing movements."[8] If this explanation is true, then the Christian Right may have attracted a core of activists who have few community ties to constrain their behavior.

In fact, most Christian Right activists are strongly attached to social and political groups. Nearly all are deeply involved in their local churches, which can provide an all-encompassing social network replete with many close friends.[9] Most are members of other conservative political groups, and many are members of professional and civic groups as well (Rozell and Wilcox, 1996). Data from the 1996 National Election Study show that core evangelicals and Christian Right supporters are both involved in more organizations than other Americans. Yet the alienation explanation does seem to fit descriptions of extremists who take extralegal actions, including killing abortion providers. These assassins are generally marginal members of groups and have frequently been expelled from their churches and from Christian Right and pro-life groups.

Group Membership As a Rational Choice

In contrast, political scientists beginning in the 1980s have generally dismissed these irrational accounts of Christian Right activism and focused instead on explanations that center on religion and politics. Most see the Christian Right as similar to all social movements, attracting primarily those individuals who share a common religious and political worldview.[10] In this sense, joining the Christian Right is as rational for Christian conservatives as is joining the Sierra Club or National Organization for Women for environmentalists and feminists.[11]

Those who join the Christian Coalition or similar groups do so because these groups articulate their religious, moral, and political sensibilities. Most activists in the Christian Right are orthodox Christians with very conservative political views. The Christian Right appeals to them because it connects their religious beliefs with their political positions.

Nevertheless, evidence that support for the Christian Right is rational does not mean that the movement is not dangerous or is good for America. Well-adjusted, rational citizens can limit the civil liberties of others and even destroy democracies.

The Christian Right and American Democracy

Critics of the Christian Right charge that it is a dangerous movement that would undermine basic civil liberties, strip rights from unpopular cultural minorities, and possibly impose a right-wing theocracy on America.[12] Of course, what appears dangerous to one American may seem perfectly reasonable to another. Direct-mail appeals by groups that oppose the Christian Right routinely begin with a warning in bold red letters that the Bill of Rights is in danger, and the fine print reveals that this danger is from a proposal to allow a moment of silence at the beginning of public school sessions in which children could pray if they wished, or meditate on a book or video game they had seen if they preferred. To some, such a moment of silence is seen as the dangerous first step down a slippery slope toward a theocracy; to others it is a basic element of religious freedom. To a pro-choice activist, the Christian Right is dangerous because it seeks to limit sharply women's reproductive freedom; to someone opposed to abortion, the abortion providers are a danger to "unborn children."

Supporters of the movement claim that the Christian Right enhances democracy by mobilizing previously apolitical Christians into active citizenship. Opponents argue that the Christian Right is dangerous because its activists do not share basic democratic norms and are not supportive of basic civil liberties. There is some truth on both claims.

Democratic Participation

Many theorists hold that democracy works best when all groups participate fully in a range of political activity. The American political system is frequently described as pluralistic—a system in which multiple, competing social and political groups bargain together within the framework of government to set public policy. When a group is disenfranchised for whatever reason, the voices of its members are not heard by the political system, and the policies produced by that system will not reflect their preferences. This is especially troubling if the members of a group hold distinctive policy positions, for if they do not participate in politics, their views do not even help shape the debate, much less public policy.

Evangelicals, pentecostals, and especially fundamentalists have traditionally been less likely to participate in politics than other citizens. Figure 4.1 shows reported white voter turnout among evangelicals and others for the 1972–1996 presidential elections. In each election, evangelical turnout was lower than that of other whites. The gap narrowed in 1992 and 1996, but in every election white evangelicals vote less often than other whites.

One reason white evangelicals vote less often than other whites is that they have lower levels of education and income, but that is only part of the explanation. Even among those with the same level of education—for example, evangelicals and nonevangelicals who have college degrees—evangelicals vote less often than other whites.

Evangelicals have traditionally been less active in politics because their religious doctrine holds that Christians should not compromise with the secular world but should remain apart from it. This is especially true for fundamentalists, whose separatism is more extreme than that of other evangelicals. The fundamentalist organizations of the 1980s faced a substantial barrier in mobilizing their constituency, precisely because many activists believed that politics was a dirty business that would inevitably corrupt those who engaged in it. One survey of members of the Indiana Moral Majority revealed that fully a quarter had been taught to shun politics, and more than two-thirds believed that "this world belonged to Satan." Although these activists were involved in a political organization, 42 percent were bothered by that involvement in politics, and an additional 15 percent had been bothered at one time. Fully 96 percent believed that Christ could come again at any time, an idea that made voting in the next election seem somewhat considerably less urgent.

Thus, the target constituency of the Christian Right has traditionally voted less often than other citizens. Moreover, the core constituency of the Christian Right has a distinctive set of policy preferences. The data in Table 4.2 show the differences between core white evangelicals and all other Americans on selected values and policy attitudes.

There are two important points to be made from these data. First, the core constituency of the Christian Right holds positions that are quite different from those of other whites. More than four in five core evangelicals would restrict abortion access to no more than those "traumatic" circumstances of rape, incest, and danger to the life of the mother; this view is held by half as many other Americans.

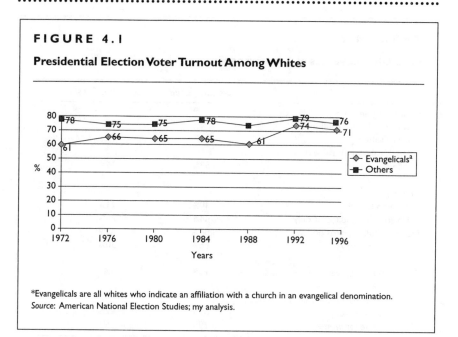

FIGURE 4.1

Presidential Election Voter Turnout Among Whites

*Evangelicals are all whites who indicate an affiliation with a church in an evangelical denomination.
Source: American National Election Studies; my analysis.

The differences are also quite large on gay rights and on the role of women. Second, even this relatively narrow core constituency does not exhibit overwhelming support for an extreme Christian Right agenda. Most of these core evangelicals would allow abortions under some circumstances, would oppose spoken prayers in the schools, and favor equal rights for women. It is not surprising, then, that the Christian Coalition has recently taken public positions that are more accommodating in these areas.

If white evangelicals have traditionally been less likely to participate in politics, and if they hold a distinctive set of issue positions, then a social movement that mobilizes them into political action might produce a more balanced and fruitful policy debate. There is ample evidence that government is responsive to those groups that participate in politics, and thus as white evangelicals become more active in politics, it is likely that policy outcomes will change.[13]

The voter turnout patterns shown in Figure 4.1 are consistent with claims by Christian Right leaders that the new organizations have been successful in mobi-

TABLE 4.2

Issue Distinctiveness of Core Evangelicals

	Core Evangelicals	Other Americans
Strongly Agree:		
Few problems if traditional family values	84%	49%
Don't tolerate those with different values	53%	24%
Abortion		
Never allowed	40%	11%
Health, rape and incest only	44%	29%
No gay antidiscrimination laws	64%	35%
No gays in military	66%	30%
Chosen school prayer	16%	9%
Mothers with young children should not		
work outside home	59%	42%
No equal role for women	29%	15%

Source: 1996 National Election Study. Core evangelicals are white members of evangelical churches, attend regularly, and hold evangelical doctrine.

lizing their target constituency into political action, although they do not constitute conclusive evidence. The gap in rates of voter turnout between white evangelicals and other whites narrowed markedly in 1992 and remained small in 1994 and 1996. In all three elections evangelicals were about as likely to vote as other whites with the same social characteristics—that is, the remaining turnout gap is entirely explained by other social characteristics of evangelicals.[14] Moreover, those evangelicals who were contacted by a religious group or who saw materials on elections at their place of worship were significantly more likely than other white evangelicals to vote in 1996, suggesting that the Christian Right's voter mobilization efforts may have had a modest impact.

Democratic Values

The American political system was designed to work by negotiation and bargaining. Factions within each body of Congress must bargain with one another, the House must bargain with the Senate, and the Congress must bargain with the president. Many critics of the Christian Right charge that it is precisely those values of bargaining and compromise that are lacking among movement activists. Instead, they charge, the Christian Right voices a moral certitude that brooks no disagreement. When activists believe that their political activity is helping to work God's will on earth, then the other side of the political discussion is distinctly *not* doing God's will. Flyers distributed in Virginia before the 1992 presidential election warned churchgoers that "a vote for Bill Clinton is a vote against God."

One northern Virginia Republican told me that when he appeared at the local caucus to help select Republican candidates for a state legislative race, a Christian Right activist asked him which candidate he was supporting. When he said he was supporting the moderate, the activist replied, "You must not be a Christian, then." The moderate Republican, who had taught Sunday school for many years in a Methodist church, was understandably appalled.

This certainty that the Christian Right is doing the will of God has obvious implications for how activists interpret the work of their political opponents. Most orthodox Christians believe that Satan is a real force in the world and is the cause of much of the social disintegration that they perceive as pandemic in America. In one survey of Moral Majority activists in Indiana, 99 percent strongly agreed that "the devil exists," nearly three in four agreed that "this world belongs to Satan," and fully 92 percent agreed that any attack on private schools "is an attack by Satan."

These beliefs were not confined to the fundamentalists of the Moral Majority. One of the most frequent themes of Christian Right direct mail in the 1990s was that public schools teach "witchcraft." The label has been especially applied to guidance counselors who attempt to implement programs that improve student self-esteem or to help students clarify their values.

Such rhetoric makes political compromise difficult, for orthodox churches preach the importance of resisting the wiles of the devil, and the Bible counsels "suffer not a witch to live."[15] It is not surprising, then, that many Christian Right activists believe that the way to deal with opponents of their policy goals is to defeat them, not to compromise with them. More than three-fourths of respondents to the survey of the Indiana Moral Majority disagreed that compromise was necessary. Among members of Christian conservative groups who attended the

Virginia Republican conventions of 1993 and 1994, only 43 percent agreed that compromise was sometimes necessary in politics, and nearly half agreed that on most matters of public policy, there was only one correct Christian view (see Table 4.3).

There is also evidence that the norms of political tolerance have not yet been well learned by Christian Right activists. One large study of religious activists found that Christian Right members most often identified liberal groups such as the National Organization for Women, the American Civil Liberties Union, and **People for the American Way** as the most dangerous to the country, and they were not especially willing to let members of such liberal groups take part in the political debate. Only 61 percent would allow them to speak in their communities, 57 percent would allow them to run for public office, 53 percent would allow them to demonstrate, and a disconcerting 14 percent would allow them to teach in public schools.[16] In contrast, although religious liberal activists frequently named the Christian Right as the greatest threat, they were far more willing to accord its adherents basic civil rights.

Research has shown that fundamentalists, pentecostals, and evangelicals—the target constituency of the Christian Right—are less tolerant of those with different political views than are other citizens: They are less willing to allow atheists, homosexuals, socialists, militarists, and racists to speak in communities, teach in colleges, or have their books available in public libraries (Wilcox and Jelen, 1990). This lack of tolerance is directly related to religious doctrine and especially to the belief in the inerrancy of the Bible. Although religious liberals and secularists may believe that all voices should be heard and tested in the marketplace of ideas, fundamentalists and other evangelicals believe that they already have the inerrant truth and that other ideas are simply wrong. They are therefore less likely to be willing to allow those ideas to be voiced because they might confuse or tempt vulnerable Christians. One study concluded, "It is not religion per se that generates intolerance, but fundamentalist theological perspectives. . . . Thus, the very motivation for [fundamentalist] political action reduces the civility of their work" (Green et al., 1994, p. 191).

It is important to note that the Christian Right elites surveyed are probably more tolerant than the average American, and that many do share the norms of compromise. Movement activists are distinctive only when compared with other political elites who share their levels of education and income. Similarly, rank-and-file fundamentalists and pentecostals are less tolerant than other Americans.

The substantial support for denying cultural liberals and secularists the right to speak, to run candidates, to demonstrate, and especially to teach in schools is troubling. If Christian activists were to gain control of the American political sys-

....

TABLE 4.3

Norms of Political Compromise (percent)

	Member of Christian Conservative Group (N = 124)	*Not a Member* (N = 316)
Compromise sometimes necessary	43	79
Neutral	21	8
Compromise not necessary	37	13
One correct Christian position	44	13
Neutral	20	12
Not one Christian position	36	75

Source: Survey of Virginia GOP delegates to 1993 and 1994 nominating conventions for details, see Rozell and Wilcox, 1996.

tem, it is possible that civil liberties for at least some Americans would be limited.[17] As I argue in the next chapter, this eventuality is unlikely, but it is significant that many Christian Right activists do not accept the civil-liberty norms of other political activists.

One important reason that Christian Right activists are more willing to deny civil liberties guarantees to liberal and secular groups is that they perceive these groups to be a major threat to America. This is not surprising given the tendency of especially the fundamentalist wing of the movement to see political battles in eschatological terms. This perception of threat is exacerbated by direct-mail publications from Christian Right groups, which darkly warn of threats and conspiracies by liberal groups. One newsletter from the Family Research Council, for example, charged that proposed rules by the federal Equal Employment Opportunity Commission (EEOC) would lead to prosecution of Christians if they wore religious jewelry, kept religious artwork on their desks, shared their faith with others during work breaks, or had a calendar with religious themes on their bulletin board.[18]

Of course, all direct mail warns of the dangers of not sending twenty-five dollars "today," and liberal groups frequently warn of great dangers to America if the

Christian Right were to "win." Yet survey data show that Christian Right activists perceive a greater threat from their political enemies than do religious liberals and appear to be more responsive to evaluations of threat than other religious activists. Consequently, Christian Right activists are more likely than others to want to deny their opponents basic civil liberties.

These data provide some support for the alarmist view that the Christian Right might pose a danger to civil liberties. Two factors may mitigate that danger, however. First, Christian Right activists, like all Americans, have internalized abstract basic democratic values and a great respect for the Constitution. They therefore hold two conflicting values: support for freedom and equality, on the one hand, and a willingness to act to protect America from moral decay, on the other. This ambivalence is not uncommon—most Americans hold conflicting values on many issues.

When Americans hold conflicting values, these values can be "primed" by political communications. This is true for Christian Right activists as well—much of the fundraising communications from movement organizations primes intolerance, but leaders sometimes prime the values of democracy. When movement leaders such as Jerry Falwell sit down with gay and lesbian activists to work on ways to lessen homophobic violence, the democratic values of movement activists may become more salient.

Second, the mere process of involvement in politics might instill in Christian Right activists a greater willingness to compromise and help to humanize their political opponents. Many political theorists have argued that the very process of participating in politics effects personal transformations among citizens. By engaging in political discourse and action, Christian conservatives may enhance their political abilities, especially what some have called their "deliberative capacities."[19] John Stuart Mill argued that participation provided moral instruction because the citizen is forced to "weigh interests not his own; to be guided, in case of conflicting claims, by another rule than his private partialities; to apply, at every turn, principles and maxims which have for their reason of existence the general good" (Mill, 1862, p. 79). Samuel Barber suggested that by debating together, citizens discover their common humanity (Barber, 1984). They may also increase their overall support for the political system and their trust in government. One study of participation in urban areas concluded that increased participation led to greater efficacy, information, and tolerance for diverse viewpoints, especially among those with lower levels of education and income (Berry, Portney, and Thomson, 1993).

Pluralists also have argued that active involvement in interest group politics tempers political passion and increases the commitment to democratic norms, such as bargaining and compromise. An activist from the Christian Coalition may work with a member of the National Rifle Association to support Oliver North, for example, and come to understand the latter's libertarian views on social issues. If that NRA member is also a member of the Sierra Club, repeated interactions may sensitize the Christian Coalition activist to the logic of environmental activists.

If these theorists are correct, the mere process of political engagement may lead to greater tolerance among Christian Right activists and greater support for democratic norms. As Christian Right activists bargain with moderate Republicans in party meetings, they learn the value of compromise. As they spend time in face-to-face dialogue with moderates, they may discover they share a concern for their children, for their communities, and for their country. As Christian conservatives enter public office, they will be forced to bargain with Democrats and in the process learn that liberals may share many of their concerns, if not their policy positions.

In Virginia, there is some indirect evidence that this process may be under way. Within the Christian Right, century-old hostilities between fundamentalists and Catholics are beginning to weaken as members of these two religious groups work together stuffing envelopes and planning strategies. One Catholic activist in Fairfax County found he was welcome in the home of fundamentalists who would have never spoken to him a decade before. Another Catholic activist spoke of the way women in the Farris campaign exchanged their views on religion and politics and of how each side came away with a renewed respect for the other's faith (Rozell and Wilcox, 1996).

Moreover, among Christian Right members in the Virginia GOP, those who have been active in politics the longest are the most willing to compromise and the least likely to believe there is one correct Christian view in politics (see Figure 4.2). Those who have been newly mobilized are far more likely to reject the necessity of political compromise and to believe there is one correct Christian view than are those who have been active for ten years or more. Presumably, two separate processes are at work: Those who remain in politics learn the norms of the process, and those who cannot compromise leave the political arena. It seems likely that some Christian Right activists from the 1980s are no longer involved in Republican politics because they were unwilling to compromise. Debra Dodson noted that "the unconventional, anticompromise style may be ill suited to sustain involvement in heterogeneous organizations that must legitimize compromise" (Dodson, 1990, p. 137).

It is by no means certain, however, that continued political involvement will lead all Christian conservative activists to greater tolerance and pragmatism. It is

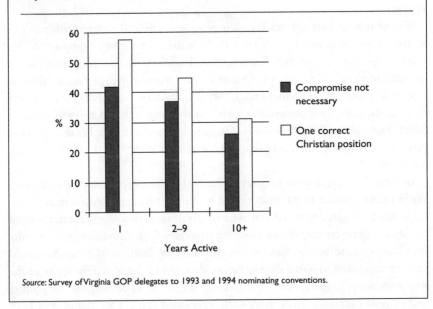

FIGURE 4.2

Norms of Compromise by Years of Activism Among Christian Right Republicans

Source: Survey of Virginia GOP delegates to 1993 and 1994 nominating conventions.

instructive that between a quarter and a third of longtime activists in Virginia reject compromise and believe that there is only one correct Christian view on political issues. These two beliefs go hand in hand, for it is difficult for people to compromise when they are certain theirs is the one "Christian" position. One study of longtime Democratic activists concluded that although party activity may socialize many "unconventional activists" into traditional norms, other of these activists may remain involved in the party despite their failure to adopt the norms of intraparty bargaining and compromise (Dodson, 1990). This appears true for the Christian Right as well.

The Christian Right Agenda

The Christian Right, like all social movements, is characterized by decentralization and has competing leaders and social movement organizations, each with somewhat different complaints and policy solutions. Nevertheless, it is possible to speak of the agenda of the movement while mindful that all activists do not support all aspects of that agenda. One place to begin to identify a Christian Right agenda is the Christian Coalition's **Contract with the American Family** (see Box 4.1), released in May 1995, soon after the House of Representatives finished its work on the Contract with America.

A majority of movement activists would probably support most of the ten planks of the Christian Coalition's contract, but this does not mean that it reflects the priorities of Christian Right activists. The contract is interesting both for what it contains and what it does not contain. Although public accommodation for religion is the first priority, abortion is fifth, after calls for abolition of the Department of Education and general support for a flat tax. Moreover, the abortion plank merely calls for limiting abortion, not for banning the procedure altogether. Not mentioned is opposition to gay rights, although this is one of the most common fundraising issues in movement mail.

Why does a central agenda document of the best-known Christian Right group merely attempt to restrict late-term abortions and not mention gay and lesbian rights? The Contract with the American Family was tested through polling and focus groups much like the Republicans' Contract with America, and this polling revealed that stronger language on abortion would weaken support for the entire package (Liebman, 1995). Only items that showed support by at least 60 percent of the population were included in the final document (Bates, 1995).

The contract was clearly intended to have broad appeal and to calm the fears of opponents of the Christian Right. It is therefore not the best statement of the agenda of movement activists but rather a political document aimed at multiple audiences. The central issues on the Christian Right agenda are abortion, education, gay rights, family values, pornography, and the role of religion in public life. In each area, movement pragmatists propose one set of policies, and more ideological elements of the Christian Right propose others. In addition, there have been efforts by Christian Right leaders to mold a consensus on economic matters.

Abortion

Although the Contract with the American Family calls only for banning some late-term abortions, most Christian Right activists believe that abortion is murder, and they ardently seek to ban most or all abortions. Speakers at the 1999 Christian Coalition convention got their most enthusiastic ovations when they called for an end to abortions. One survey of contributors to Pat Robertson's presidential campaign found that over 91 percent agreed that abortion should be banned (Brown, Powell, and Wilcox, 1995); in another survey of members of

BOX 4.1

The Christian Coalition's Contract with the American Family

1. Allow communal prayer in public places such as schools, high school graduation ceremonies, and courthouses.

2. Abolish the federal Department of Education.

3. Establish vouchers for parents to use to send their children to private and parochial schools.

4. Establish a $500 tax credit for children, favor "in concept" a flat tax, remove the "marriage penalty" in tax laws, and allow homemakers to contribute $2,000 annually toward an Individual Retirement Account.

5. Limit abortion, ban certain abortion procedures, end use of Medicaid funds for abortion, cut off federal funding for groups such as Planned Parenthood.

6. Limit access to pornography on cable television and the Internet.

7. Abolish federal funding for the National Endowments for the Arts and Humanities, the Corporation for Public Broadcasting, and the Legal Services Corporation.

8. Eventually turn over welfare programs to private charities.

9. Enact a "Parental Rights Act" and reject the U.N. Convention on the Rights of the Child.

10. Use federal funds to encourage states to require prisoners to study and work and require restitution to victims subsequent to release.

Source: Washington Post, May 18, 1995, p. A6.

Christian Right groups at the 1993 and 1994 Virginia Republican nominating conventions, 82 percent agreed that abortions should be prohibited (Rozell and Wilcox, 1996).

Most activists regard abortion as the slaughter of the innocents and would therefore ban abortion altogether except in those few instances when the life of the mother is truly in danger. Many would not allow abortion even then and would argue that God should make the ultimate decision.[20] For a few committed activists, abortion is murder, and abortion providers are murderers who should be treated as such. One prominent fundamentalist Bible study guide, in its discussion of Exodus 21, reached the dubious conclusion that the Bible called for the death penalty for abortion providers.[21]

It is a measure of just how strong the pro-life consensus is in the Christian Right that activists will only voice their qualms on the issue off the record. One activist in Ohio made me turn off my tape recorder and promise never to reveal her responses to other Moral Majority members, then told me that she supported an exception for rape because she had been raped a few years before and had worried for weeks about a possible pregnancy. Another Virginia man with a wife in uncertain health privately endorsed an exception for maternal health, but he too repeatedly asked that I tell no one else in the movement of his views.

These activists may not be as isolated as they think, for a survey of Indiana Moral Majority members in 1982 found that nearly one in five approved of abortions in cases of rape, and more than half approved of abortions when the woman's life was in danger. A survey of the membership of Concerned Women of America conducted in the 1980s showed that 65 percent of the organization's members would allow abortions to save the life of the mother, and 21 percent would additionally allow abortions in cases of rape and incest (Blakeman, nd). Yet precisely these kinds of issues provoke heated debates in Christian Right circles, and the movement does not want those debates to be held publicly. Perhaps for this reason, Christian Right speakers use consensual language such as "protecting the life of the unborn" rather than focusing on any specific exceptions that should be granted.

Although most Americans are uncomfortable with abortions, they are even more uncomfortable with allowing the government to determine when women may obtain them. Surveys consistently show that only a small minority of Americans favor banning all abortions, and they are far outnumbered by those who favor allowing abortions for all adult women (Cook, Jelen, and Wilcox, 1992). The public is evenly divided between those who would restrict abortion to the "traumatic" circumstances of danger to the life or health of the mother, rape, and fetal defect and those who would allow abortion in most circumstances.

Although the Republican party embraced a pro-life plank in its 1980 presidential platform and has kept it in all elections since, there is evidence that the abortion issue hurt Republicans in the 1992 election (Abramowitz, 1995). There is a strong consensus in America in favor of some restrictions on abortion (for example, requiring teenage girls to notify a parent before having an abortion or requiring a woman to wait twenty-four hours before the procedure is performed), but there is strong opposition to banning all abortions. Candidates who support an outright ban on abortions lose if the election turns on that issue (Cook, Jelen, and Wilcox, 1994).

Some movement leaders appear to believe that it is better to elect candidates who will impose modest procedural restrictions on access to abortion than to fight elections over an abortion ban and lose. Movement activists are sharply divided over strategy on abortion—pragmatism or purity. Many Christian Right leaders promote the former in the belief that it is possible in the United States today to win passage of restrictions on abortion access but it is not possible to ban abortions. In a November 4, 1993, appearance on ABC's *Nightline*, Pat Robertson explained: "I would urge people, as a matter of private choice, not to choose abortion, because I think it is wrong. It's something else, though, in the political arena to go out on a quixotic crusade when you know you'll be beaten continuously. So I say let's do what is possible. What is possible is parental consent."[22]

Despite this pragmatic announcement, Robertson has sent mixed signals on abortion over the past five years. Although he has sometimes indicated a willingness to support candidates who merely support additional restrictions on abortion, he also denounced GOP presidential candidate Bob Dole's announcement that he no longer supported a constitutional amendment to ban abortion. In response, *Washington Post* cartoonist Herblock drew Dole sitting on a stool while hooded Christian Coalition members brought wood to burn him for heresy. In 1999, Robertson signaled that he found acceptable George W. Bush's position on abortion—to push for laws criminalizing certain late-term procedures and to impose other restrictions without an outright ban. Bush has refused to endorse a litmus test on abortion for Supreme Court nominees, but has called for laws to protect the unborn.

Education

Education issues rival abortion in their ability to mobilize Christian Right enthusiasts. At the Christian Coalition convention in 1999, some of the loudest cheers came when speakers called for eliminating the federal Department of Education and abolishing various programs of national educational standards such as Goals 2000 and outcomes-based education. In Ohio in the early 1980s, the Christian schools group was far larger than the Moral Majority, and Michael Farris surprised many observers by mobilizing thousands of homeschool advocates to attend the 1993 Virginia Republican nominating convention and select him as nominee for lieutenant governor.

At the heart of Christian Right criticism of American education is the charge that it promotes anti-Christian values and threatens the ability of conservative Christians to inculcate their values in their own children. The specifics of this critique are diverse. Many argue that the schools promote a religion called **secular**

humanism, a doctrine that places humans at the center of the universe with no room for God. Others single out multicultural curricula, which promote tolerance for non-Christian lifestyles. Still others decry classes that invite students to clarify their values, for they fear that this clarity may lead some to reject their orthodox Christian views. Many Christian Right activists focus their attention on school psychologists, who they believe "brainwash" students away from their Christian values. All bemoan the absence of prayer and religious content in the schools.

For some Christian Right activists, the public schools are a lost cause, and Christian parents must educate their children at home or in religious schools. Michael Farris, for example, in exasperation after a court ruling against parents who sought to remove their children from parts of the public school curriculum, proclaimed that "it is time for every born-again Christian to get their children out of public schools."[23] The alternatives promoted by the Christian Right are religious schools, often associated with fundamentalist or Catholic churches, and homeschool education.[24]

Christian Right activists who promote homeschooling and Christian schools have their own agenda. The central objective is tax relief, for they resent paying taxes to support public schools and then paying to educate their children outside those schools. They also vehemently resist state regulation of the content of this education or of the credentials of those who teach it. All enthusiastically support proposals for tuition tax credits and especially for educational vouchers, which would give each family a voucher to be used to purchase whatever kind of education the family desired.

Other activists keep their children in the public schools and fight battles to alter the curriculum. Some seek to teach creationism in addition to or in place of evolution, to teach only the virtues of abstinence in sex education classes, and to teach the Bible as literature. Others attempt to excuse their children from reading certain books or attending sex education classes. Most seek to include prayer in public schools, although some would have only a moment of silent prayer, others a voluntary spoken prayer, and a small minority a mandatory spoken prayer. All seek more local control of the school curriculum, since a small number of motivated activists can often greatly affect the outcome of educational battles at the local level. Most Christian Right organizations have opposed efforts to establish national educational standards. Many activists believe that these programs would establish a national curriculum that promotes secular humanism and values clarification.

Many Christian conservatives believe that education policy at the national level is set by a group of liberal counterculture activists whose values are outside of the

American mainstream. On the campaign trail, presidential candidate Patrick Buchanan gets great cheers from Christian Right activists by railing against policymakers from the Department of Education who wore "beads and sandals," a reference to the attire of the "hippies" of the 1960s. Because these liberals are seen as dominating the education establishment, activists believe that it is essential that Christian parents get some control of local school boards. The number of Christian Right candidacies for school board races is increasing rapidly (Deckman, 1999).

Among members of Christian Right groups who attended Virginia Republican nominating conventions, 80 percent believed that the government should promote homeschooling and that the public schools should be required to teach creationism as an alternative to evolution. Nearly two-thirds of those who gave money to Pat Robertson's presidential campaign favored a mandatory prayer in public schools.

Some elements of the Christian Right agenda for education are quite popular with the public; others strike most Americans as extreme and perhaps dangerous. A clear majority of Americans favor a moment of silence during which children can pray if they wish, though most Americans oppose a chosen, spoken prayer in schools. A majority of Americans also favor teaching creationism along with evolution, although the survey data do not reveal whether they would want both theories taught as being equally plausible.[25] And a majority of Americans want high school sex education courses to encourage abstinence and discourage homosexual behavior.

Yet a substantial majority of Americans favor teaching about birth control in classrooms and teaching ways to prevent the spread of AIDS and other diseases. They also want their schools to encourage independent thinking on politics, economics, and moral issues. And many are frightened of the extreme rhetoric of some Christian conservatives, who charge that schools teach "witchcraft" and seek to remove books such as *The Wizard of Oz* from the classroom because it contains an account of a "good witch."

Opposition to Gay and Lesbian Rights

Although homosexuality was not mentioned in the Contract with the American Family, opposition to it is a key part of the agenda of all Christian Right groups and an important focus for their direct-mail fundraising. Christian Right activists perceive that educators, the media elite, and other liberals are trying to legitimate a "radical homosexual rights agenda." One Christian Right direct-mail appeal charged that liberals would seek to mandate that churches and schools hire "known, practicing, soliciting homosexual teachers" and teach children in public schools how to engage in homosexual behavior.

Christian Right activists believe that homosexual conduct is sinful—for many it is far more sinful than adultery or fornication and was the reason that God destroyed two cities in biblical times. Yet although the Bible promises that children raised in the faith will not stray from it, many activists know conservative Christians with gay or lesbian children—indeed one son of a prominent Christian Right leader came out in the early 1990s. This leads many activists to believe that gays and lesbians seduce heterosexuals and that the gay and lesbian lifestyle is powerfully attractive.

All activists oppose any public legitimation of gays and lesbians. They object to sympathetic portraits of gays on television, in books, and especially in the classroom. Some have gone so far as to seek to remove from school libraries any books that mention homosexuality without condemning it, under the assumption that if adolescents are exposed to even the idea of homosexuality, they will be strongly drawn to experiment.[26]

In addition, Christian Right organizations universally condemn any national, state, or local laws that prohibit discrimination against gays and lesbians in housing and employment. Currently in many states it is legal to fire an employee discovered to be gay, regardless of the quality of the person's work in the company, and to refuse to rent to or in some cases even to evict gay and lesbian tenants. In some states and an increasing number of cities and counties, laws that ban such discrimination have been considered and sometimes passed. The Christian Right fights such laws.

The antidiscrimination laws are usually referred to within the movement as conferring "special rights" on gays and lesbians. Some Christian Right activists seek to frame their opposition to laws protecting the civil rights of gays and lesbians as an effort to protect the rights of conservative Christians. Tony Marco, a leading strategist in the movement to limit gay and lesbian rights through amendments to state constitutions, has argued that "law [should not] constrain Christians or anyone else from exercising where appropriate their freedoms . . . i.e., not forcing them to hire or promote anyone based solely on their alleged homosexual orientation" (cited in Morken, 1994). Thus, when gay and lesbian activists seek to pass laws to protect them from job discrimination, Christian Right activists respond that such laws would force them to hire gays and lesbians in violation of their religious beliefs.[27]

Many Christian Right activists argue that homosexual *behavior* is sinful but that Christians should "hate the sin, love the sinner." They strongly reject the implications of recent research that there may be a genetic component to homosexuality and believe instead that sexual orientation is entirely a voluntary choice.[28] The Christian Regeneration Ministries seeks to "convert" gays and lesbians to heterosexuality, and many Christian Right activists believe that such ministries offer a "solution" to the "gay problem." In 1998 and 1999, Focus on the Family and other Christian Right groups launched a massive campaign to promote conversion of gays and lesbians (Millsaps, 1999). The "Truth in Love" campaign had several goals: to redefine the public debate on homosexuality, to remind movement activists that they were to love gays and lesbians and try to lead them to salvation, and to convince gays and lesbians to attempt to change their lifestyle.

Other activists clearly hate the "sinner" as well. One segment of the Christian Right is strongly homophobic. When Mark Rozell and I surveyed Republican activists in Virginia, some Christian Right activists penciled in vicious comments beside our questions about gay rights. Three quoted Old Testament proscriptions of homosexual behavior that mandated death by stoning for homosexuals. These activists were a minority and were in fact more than matched by others who wrote in nuanced comments that they merely wanted to stop public displays of homosexuality, not to ferret out closeted gays and lesbians.

In 1999, many gay and lesbian activists charged that inflammatory rhetoric by the Christian Right contributed to an atmosphere of homophobia that led to a series of hate crime assaults and murders. In response, the Moral Majority founder, Jerry Falwell, staged a public meeting with gay and lesbian evangelicals (including his own former ghostwriter) and promised to change the language in his fundraising appeals.

Although there is a consensus among Christian Right activists that the culture should not promote homosexuality as a legitimate lifestyle, there are divisions in the movement about just how central the issue should be to the Christian Right agenda and how far to go in discouraging homosexual conduct. Among Christian Right activists who attended Virginia Republican nominating conventions in 1993 and 1994, nearly 90 percent opposed allowing gays and lesbians to teach in public schools, and nearly a third favored prosecuting known homosexuals. Yet more than 40 percent opposed such prosecutions. Fully 98 percent of members of the Indiana Moral Majority wanted to fire public school teachers if they were discovered to be homosexual.

The American public is also divided on gay rights. One national survey in 1996 found that a majority of Americans were uncomfortable with the thought of homosexuality, and a third were strongly disgusted. Nearly half believed that homosexual relations are unnatural. This ambivalence was also evident in attitudes on policy items. A majority favored laws to prohibit discrimination against gays, and a majority also favored allowing gays and lesbians to serve openly in the military.

Yet an even larger majority opposed allowing gays and lesbians to adopt children (Wilcox and Wolpert, 2000).

Traditional Families

Many Christian Right leaders refer to their groups as **pro-family,** for obvious reasons. Families are positive symbols to Americans, and most people, liberal or conservative, believe that the policies they favor would help American families. Many Christian Right activists go further and advocate policies that would promote "traditional" families. The central issue is the role of women in society and of children's and parent's rights.

The ideal family for many Christian conservatives is a married couple with children, the father working for wages outside the home and the mother working as a homemaker, at least while her children are young. Christian Right activists charge that government policy encourages women to work, both by providing tax breaks for child care for working mothers and by allowing homemakers to contribute only a small amount toward individual retirement accounts (IRAs). Moreover, they charge that high taxes are the primary reason that women enter the workforce, and many argue that lowering taxes would encourage women to stay at home and tend to their children.[29] Many are critical of county-funded after-school child care, charging that it encourages women to work outside the home.

For some fundamentalists and other conservative evangelicals, the Bible prescribes specific roles for women and men in families, with the man as the head of the household (Ammerman, 1987). Women and men are thought to have different abilities and strengths, which make each specially suited to certain tasks. Televangelists frequently preach on the theme of a woman's role in the family as mother, homemaker, and supporter of her husband. Some Christian Right activists take this division of labor very seriously: Among the delegates who supported Michael Farris in his bid for the Virginia GOP nomination for lieutenant governor were a number of men whose wives were not delegates because this was not a proper role for women. Instead, many of these women arranged for babysitting for other Farris delegates. Fully a third of Farris delegates believed that men are better suited for politics than are women, and 90 percent of the members of the Indiana Moral Majority indicated that they believed in male-dominated families.

A larger number of Christian Right activists believe that women should play an active and equal part in politics but that because they also have special abilities as mothers, they should remain in the home while their children are young. Among Christian Right delegates in the Virginia GOP, a substantial majority believed that women who worked outside the home could not establish as warm and nurturing a relationship with their children as those women who stayed home full-time. It is small wonder that housewives and those who worked only part-time in the paid labor force constituted a substantial majority of women who were Christian Right delegates.

Christian conservatives also object to any government interference in how they raise their children, including in matters of discipline. Many fundamentalists and other evangelicals believe that God has prescribed physical punishment as the optimal form of discipline, and courts in many states are drawing increasingly strict definitions of child abuse. The Christian Right objects to such limitations and also seeks to overturn state laws and policies that might force disturbed children to receive counseling or that might remove children from homes under a variety of circumstances. Michael Farris has written a novel depicting the dangers of such laws when the state tries to remove a child from a Christian home because of an anonymous accusation of child abuse. A few Christian conservatives have also objected to laws that specifically criminalize spousal abuse, including rape within marriage and spousal beating, and have urged the government to stop funding spousal abuse centers.[30]

An overwhelming majority of Americans agree that America would be better off if there were more attention to family values. Yet most also support an equal role for women in politics and in the larger society. Fully 91 percent of respondents in recent surveys indicate that they would vote for a woman for president if she was from their party and shared their views. There is also substantial support for gender equality in families: A clear majority of Americans disagree that the man should be the achiever outside the home while the woman takes care of the home and family and that the husband's career is more important than the wife's career. A majority believe that working mothers can establish just as warm and secure a relationship with their children as can homemakers and that preschool children do not suffer if the mother works. Yet a sizable minority of Americans disagree on these issues and believe that mothers should remain at home, especially before their children enter school.[31]

The pro-family label of the Christian Right deeply angers liberals, who complain that many of the economic policies advocated by Christian Right leaders, including privatizing welfare programs and reducing spending on Medicaid, hurt working families. They also complain that the Christian Right's definition of a family is far too narrow and that single mothers and nontraditional families can provide loving environments for children. Finally, they argue that the Christian Right's strong opposition to gay and lesbian rights and the opposition by some in the movement to laws that protect women and children from physical abuse clearly harm some members of some families. A bumper sticker frequently seen in the Washington, D.C., area is "Hate Is Not a Family Value." As Focus on the Family has become more powerful, a new bumper sticker advises Christian Right activists to "Focus on Your Own Damn Family."

Pornography

Conservative Christians have long sought to limit access by children and adults alike to erotic literature and images, and the Christian Right today wants to restrict the distribution and possession of "pornography." The greatest issue for many activists is the easy access to hard-core pornography provided by the Internet: one mother told me of doing a Yahoo search with her child for monster pictures for Halloween, and getting links to three sites of hard-core images and videos. The Christian Coalition advocates stronger legislation on child pornography and has backed proposed legislation to ban pornography from the Internet, and countless local groups seek to remove from their public libraries books and newspapers that they find offensive or to stop the sale of adult magazines in their community.

It is often argued that pornography is difficult to define but easy to recognize. This may be true in some instances, but pornography is also in the eye of the beholder, and Americans in general vary widely in what they label pornographic. Some find *Playboy* magazine pornographic. Others might reserve such a label for *Hustler*, and still others might object only to hard-core magazines and films that actually depict sexual acts. Some feel library books that sympathetically portray a lesbian romance are pornographic, and others object to any books that contain pictures of nude men or women, even as paintings in art books.

Christian Right activists are also divided on these matters and advocate different policies. Some would limit all kinds of erotic materials and ban not only their production and distribution but also their ownership. Others would limit only the sale and distribution of hard-core sexual materials, such as XXX-rated movies and magazines and Internet pictures that depict explicit sex acts. Still others seek primarily to keep adult materials out of the hands of children.

Surveys of Christian Right activists reveal that sizable majorities favor limiting adult access to sexually explicit materials. Large majorities of Christian Right activists surveyed in Fairfax County, Virginia, favored limiting adult access to pornography, as did 75 percent of contributors to Pat Robertson's presidential campaign.[32] Fully 70 percent of Fairfax activists favored establishing an adults-only section of the public library, and another 16 percent strongly opposed such a policy and wrote on the survey that the books should be removed from the library altogether.

The public is ambivalent about limitations on pornography. A majority favors banning the distribution of pornographic materials to those under eighteen, and a sizable minority favors banning distribution to adults as well. Majorities believe that sexual materials lead people to commit rape and lead to a breakdown in public morals, but a majority also believes that sexual materials provide an outlet for bottled-up sexual urges.

Interestingly, the pornography issue is one on which the Christian Right finds common ground with many feminists, who believe that sexually explicit films and magazines exploit women and may lead to sexual violence. But many libertarian conservatives oppose the Christian Right on this issue, holding that adults should have the right to read whatever they choose. Proposals by the more ideological elements of the Christian Right movement to remove any book from the public library that describes a sexual encounter, including many best-selling novels, lead many to charge that the Christian Right is a movement of book-burning moral censors.

A Christian Nation

Most Christian Right activists seek to restore a more public role for religion in general and Christianity in particular in American life. Most Christian Right activists believe that their religion is denigrated by modern society, government, and the media, and that God will not continue to smile on a nation that marginalizes Christianity. They note that born-again Christians constitute more than one quarter of the national population, but do not appear as sympathetic characters (or really at all) on network programming.

The first element in the Contract with the American Family was a proposed Religious Equality Amendment to the U.S. Constitution. The Christian Coalition's pamphlet on the contract cites a variety of "wrongs" the amendment is intended to correct, many stemming from misinterpretations by overly zealous school administrators of court rulings about separation of church and state. The pamphlet cites several examples: a schoolgirl in Nevada banned from singing "The First Noel" at a Christmas pageant, bans on religious celebrations in Scarsdale, New York, public schools, children told they cannot read the Bible in study time, nativity scenes barred from post offices, and courthouses banned from displaying the Ten Commandments.

Most activists clearly intend for prayers in schools to be Christian prayers and the public displays of religion to be Christian ones. Although many Christian

Right activists would allow displays of the menorah in December and might accept secular symbols such as Santa Claus as well, they are primarily interested in displays of the nativity scene. Some will even privately admit that they are not especially comfortable with displays of the menorah, much less a statue of Buddha or Vishnu, on the courthouse lawn.

Because of this, many opponents charge that the Christian Right seeks to create a truly "Christian nation," in which religious minorities would be at best marginalized and perhaps forced to participate in Christian religious activities. The leadership of the Christian Coalition has gone to great lengths to calm such fears: Ralph Reed denied explicitly that the group sought to establish an exclusively Christian nation and pointedly included Jews and occasionally Muslims as the "people of faith" discriminated against by American culture (Reed, 1994a).

Yet not all Christian Right activists are so inclusive. Research shows that evangelicals (and others) are uncomfortable with public displays of non-Christian religion and are especially unwilling to have their children exposed to such displays in the classroom. As noted previously, nearly two-thirds of Robertson's donors supported a mandatory spoken school prayer, as did a third of Christian Right activists at the Virginia Republican conventions. For many activists, imposing Christianity on nonbelievers merely increases the odds that their souls will spend eternity in heaven.

In Arizona, Christian Right activists who attended a Republican state convention passed a floor resolution declaring that the United States was a Christian nation and that the Constitution created "a republic based upon the absolute laws of the Bible, not a democracy."[33] Similar motions have failed in other states, such as Georgia, but have had strong support by Christian conservatives. The Reverend Tim LaHaye, a prominent movement writer, has repeatedly argued that humanists are not fit to hold positions of government and should be removed.

At the fringe of the Christian Right is a group of theorists who adhere to the doctrine of **Christian reconstructionism.** Also known as dominion theologists, kingdom theologians, or theonomists, these reconstructionists are postmillennialists who believe that Christians must work to recover control of America from the forces of Satan in order to establish the millennium and allow Christ to come again. To do this requires that society be reconstructed from the ground up, generally in keeping with Mosaic law (the laws of Moses) as detailed in the first five books of the Bible.

Rousas John Rushdoony, the most influential reconstructionist thinker, has said that a reconstructed America would have no room for Jews, Buddhists, Muslims, Hindus, Bahais, or humanists. There might not even be room for nonreconstructed Christians, for Christian reconstructionists seek to dominate society. According to Gary North, a leading reconstructionist writer, it is important to adopt the language of liberalism until the reconstruction has begun, but after that time, there is no reason to tolerate dissent.

Perhaps most controversial is the reconstructionists' call for capital punishment to be meted out according to Mosaic law—to those who murder, commit adultery, engage in homosexual behavior, act incorrigibly as teenagers, blaspheme, or commit acts of apostasy. North has claimed that death by stoning not only is an important part of the Mosaic code but also has certain advantages: Stones are plentiful and cheap, no single "killing blow" can be traced to any individual, and group stone-throwing underscores the community norms being enforced.[34]

It must be noted that Christian reconstructionists are but a tiny fringe of the Christian Right, but their arguments are being increasingly incorporated in mainstream writing, including in books by Pat Robertson (Shupe, 1989). This does not mean that many Christian Right activists advocate stoning incorrigible children, but it does indicate that serious discussions are taking place among Christian Right activists of how to go about restructuring society to conform with biblical law.

Public opinion polls suggest that Americans are generally supportive of a greater role for religion in public life and are at least somewhat willing to accommodate the needs of non-Christian groups. One national survey in 1989 showed that large majorities of Americans favored a prayer to open sessions of Congress and before high school sporting events, a moment of silence in schools, displays of nativity scenes and menorahs on public land, allowing student religious groups to meet on school property, and teaching creationism in addition to evolution in schools (Jelen and Wilcox, 1995).

Yet focus groups conducted by Ted Jelen revealed a more complex picture. Most of those who participated in these groups were initially unable to imagine why issues such as prayer in schools were controversial. When asked how children from minority religious traditions might react, they suggested nonsectarian prayers. When asked how Buddhist or Muslim children might react, they expressed more discomfort but indicated that these children could simply leave the room. Yet when other participants pointed out that this would stigmatize the students, many became uneasy. And when Jelen suggested that a truly neutral prayer might need to rotate across religious traditions, no parents were willing to have their children sit through a Buddhist prayer (Jelen and Wilcox, 1995).

Nonetheless, the Christian Coalition's agenda on public accommodation of religion is generally popular. Once again, however, the policy proposals of the more radical elements of the movement frighten not only Jews and other non-Christians but many evangelicals as well.

An Economic Agenda?

Beginning with the fundamentalist groups of the 1980s, Christian Right leaders have tried to develop an economic agenda. Although the target audience for the movement is less affluent than are other Americans, various Christian Right groups have endorsed subminimum wages, a return to the gold standard, protectionist trade policies, privatizing the welfare system, cuts in Medicaid and other social spending, and a flat income tax. They have also opposed President Clinton's proposed 4.5-cent gasoline tax and national health insurance. Many of these policies would likely hurt poor families while helping affluent Americans.

The economic elements of the Christian Right agenda have received a mixed reception among movement activists. There is a sizable core of movement activists who agree with all of these economic policy positions and back the expanded agenda with enthusiasm. Others agree with the policy positions but feel uncomfortable advocating them within the context of organizations that claim a Christian mandate. These activists argue that the social issue agenda on abortion, gay rights, and school curricula should be central to the movement. Others are neutral toward the policies and take a pragmatic stand: They will support the policy concerns of economic conservatives if the economic conservatives will in turn back the social agenda of the Christian Right.

Yet a number of activists are troubled by the economic positions of the Christian Right. One Catholic activist in northern Virginia told me that she interpreted the Bible to indicate a great sympathy for the poor and that cuts in welfare spending might lead to more abortions by poor women. Another activist told me that he believed the Christian Coalition had become too enamored of policies to help the rich, although Christ had warned that "a rich man shall hardly enter into the kingdom of heaven. . . . It is easier for a camel to go through the eye of a needle, than for a rich man to enter into the kingdom of heaven."[35]

Surveys show that white evangelicals have a mixed reaction to the economic agenda of the Christian Right. Calls to eliminate welfare and to scale back other poverty programs appeal to the economic individualism rooted in the Calvinist heritage of evangelicals, but even those who take conservative positions on these issues do not see them as essentially religious questions. Other white evangelicals favor government action to provide aid to the poor.

The economic agenda may pose a barrier to greater expansion of the Christian Right among conservative Catholics because their communitarian ethic does not mesh well with calls to eliminate welfare and scale back other poverty programs. Moreover, many Catholics believe that the danger of such cuts increasing abortions by poor women is sufficiently great that they oppose any reductions in aid for the poor. The economic agenda is an even greater barrier to mobilizing black evangelicals, who generally support government aid to the poor.

The Agenda As Defensive Action

The core elements of the Christian Right agenda are reactions against the social change of the past several decades. The successes of other groups—of feminists on abortion and gender equality, of gays and lesbians in gaining social and legal acceptance, of the environmental movement in protecting endangered species, of educational reformers in promoting courses to help children think about values and improve their self-esteem—have sparked a reaction by conservative Christians who preferred the policies of the past. The progress made by liberal groups in these policy areas threatens the worldview of conservative Christians and appears to them to have been possible only because of an almost conspiratorial alliance of liberal forces. For this reason, many Christian Right activists refer to even their policies on abortion, gay rights, and the environment as defensive.

Indeed, many argue that this agenda is necessary to protect their children and families from dangerous temptations. Many Christian Right activists do not especially care if other women work, but they seek tax and retirement policies that enable conservative Christian women to stay home with children. They object to public acceptance of gays and lesbians because they fear their children will be attracted to the lifestyle, and they reserve their greatest energies for battles over the education of their children. They object to television networks that portray lifestyles that they believe are sinful as sympathetic characters, yet fail to portray sympathetic evangelical Christian characters.

Yet feminists, environmentalists, gays and lesbians, and educators see these same policies as an attempt to impose an outdated lifestyle on all citizens. One bumper sticker common in the Washington, D.C., suburbs captures this sentiment: "IF YOU OPPOSE ABORTION DON'T HAVE ONE." Gays and lesbians who face discrimination, insults, and even hate crimes see the Christian Right's efforts as an attempt to force them back into the closet.

For each element of the Christian Right agenda, the policies advocated by movement moderates hold appeal for at least a sizable minority of Americans. Those policies advocated by the more ideological elements of the movement attract support from only a small minority, however, and are passionately opposed by a large number of citizens. Policies advocated by the more ideological fringe of the Christian Right frighten most Americans and provide the evidentiary basis for the most extreme stereotypes of movement activists.

The extreme positions and statements by the fringe elements of the Christian Right movement are not unusual, for all movements attract members who vary in their ideological purity and their willingness to compromise. The civil rights movement in the 1960s attracted pastors who preached nonviolence and Black Panthers who distributed coloring books showing black children killing police officers. The environmental movement includes those who seek to lobby Congress to protect wilderness areas and those who advocate destruction of the equipment used by those who would ravage the earth.

Yet anyone evaluating the Christian Right must ultimately choose which of the various factions within the movement is likely to dominate in the future, and much depends on that answer. If moderates predominate, the movement likely will be sizable, and its issue agenda will be partially realized. If radicals such as the Christian reconstructionists come to represent the movement, the movement likely will be marginalized, and its agenda strongly repudiated.

Conclusion

Is the Christian Right a democratic force that is engaging a previously apolitical segment of the public in political action, or is it a dangerous force that will limit civil liberties? In this chapter I have posed several questions in an effort to address this larger issue.

First, is support for the Christian Right concentrated among individuals with authoritarian personalities? Although sociologists of the 1950s posited that supporters of the Right must have dysfunctional personalities or be deeply alienated from society, there is little evidence that this is true for the Christian Right. Instead, support for the movement appears to be a politically rational choice of conservative Christians to join groups that will advance their favored policies.

Second, has the Christian Right expanded the pluralist system in America by mobilizing previously apolitical groups? The evidence suggests that the target constituents of the Christian Right have historically been less likely than other citizens to participate in politics and that they do hold distinctive policy views. Should the Christian Right finally succeed in mobilizing these citizens into politics and in securing for them a voice in policy discussions, the policy debate will be more inclusive.

Third, do Christian Right activists advocate limiting civil rights? Here the evidence is mixed, and the answer nuanced. A majority of Christian Right activists would extend most basic civil liberties to their opponents, but they are much less likely to do so than other elites. Only a few Christian Right activists would arrest known homosexuals in their homes, but many seek to overturn laws that protect homosexuals from being fired simply because of their sexual orientation. Only a very few Christian Right activists would deny women the right to work outside the home, but many seek to eliminate programs that make it easier for them to enter the workplace and call for financial incentives for women to remain in the home. Only a few Christian Right activists would advocate wholesale firings of teachers who are liberal or feminist, but a majority oppose hiring gays and lesbians, feminists, and even liberals. In each case, movement extremists advocate policies that would mean a severe curtailment of civil liberties, and a majority of activists would limit the lifestyle options of cultural liberals.

Finally, is the agenda of the Christian Right a mainstream agenda, as movement leaders claim, or a radical one, as the movement's opponents charge? Here again the answer is complex, for in each policy area movement pragmatists propose policies that have at least some broad appeal, and movement ideologues propose policies that frighten and repel many Americans.

Thus, the answer to the question of whether the Christian Right is good or bad for America depends on what role the movement plays in the future and which faction within the movement comes to dominate. In the next chapter I consider the future of the Christian Right.

5

....

The Future of
the Christian Right

The conclusion is that the New Christian Right will fail
. . . both to re-Christianize America and to prevent
further displacement of the values which its supporters
hold dear.

—Steve Bruce,
The Rise and Fall of the New Christian Right, p. 192

The Christian Right has been adaptable and innovative.
It will do well in the twenty-first century precisely
because it will discover ways to balance its increasing
political moderation with its fixed religious principles.

—Matthew Moen,
"The Christian Right in the Twenty-first Century"

A̲FTER CLARENCE DARROW EMBARRASSED William Jennings Bryan in the Scopes trial, many observers thought fundamentalism was finished. H. L. Mencken, writing in the *Baltimore Sun*, described fundamentalists variously as "yokels," "half-wits," "gaping primates," "anthropoid rabble," "morons," and "inquisitors" and predicted their eventual extinction. After the trial, it was accepted wisdom that the fundamentalists had lost their battle with modernism and would be forever vanquished by progress and science.

This prediction proved to be far from the mark. In 1981 journalists declared that the fundamentalist Moral Majority was one of the most important forces in American politics and that its agenda was soon to be realized by the newly elected Republican president and Senate. When Pat Robertson launched his presidential bid in 1987, some sociologists argued that he might win the presidency because of the vast numbers of evangelicals, fundamentalists, and charismatics who would rally to his campaign.

These predictions were also in error, for the Moral Majority accomplished little, and Robertson lost badly. In 1989 it appeared that the third wave of the Christian Right had spent its energies and that evangelicals would again retreat to privatized religious faith. Moral Majority's founder, Jerry Falwell, was immensely unpopular, and his organization was bankrupt. Pat Robertson had been embarrassed during his campaign and was trying to salvage his television empire from its dire financial straits. Many predicted that the Christian Right was defeated and that evangelicals would again retreat into their private religious world.

In the early 1990s, many predicted that the Christian Right would soon take over the Republican party entirely and begin to influence national politics in a major way. Although the movement has achieved substantial influence in the party, its policy achievements have been few and far between. By 1999, some were proclaiming the death of the movement that just a few years earlier they had described as a juggernaut.

Clearly, predictions about the future of the Christian Right have great potential to embarrass those bold enough to venture them. For many of the fundamentalists and pentecostals of the Christian Right, the twenty-first century promises great hope. Many believe that the new millennium will usher in the biblical millennium, in which Christ will come again. As noted by political scientist Michael

Lienesch, "As the twentieth century approaches its conclusion, these religious conservatives look anxiously and eagerly toward the twenty-first, predicting catastrophic events and world-redeeming wonders. . . . all agree that the sweeping transformations of the late twentieth century. . . appear to be highly prophetic, suggesting in one form or another the end of the existing world and the beginning of a new one" (Lienesch, 1994, pp. 245–246). Pat Robertson has modestly predicted the second coming of Christ on April 29, 2007—Robertson's seventy-seventh birthday.[1]

Political scientists differ considerably in their views of the future of the movement. Credible scholars now predict the "inevitable failure" of the Christian Right, but others foresee considerable growth and institutionalization for the movement. These disparate reflections reflect different assessments of the strengths and weaknesses of the movement and, in some cases, some wishful thinking by its opponents and supporters.

In this chapter I consider two specific questions about the future of the Christian Right and then risk some tentative predictions about the movement in the twenty-first century.

Can the Christian Right Expand?

Surveys in the 1980s showed that the Moral Majority commanded the support of approximately 25 percent of white evangelicals, most of them among the fundamentalist wing of the community. One large national survey in 1996 showed that the Christian Coalition and similar groups in the 1990s were far more popular, with 55 percent of white evangelicals rating the Christian Right favorably (Green, 1996; but see Wilcox, DeBell and Sigelman, 1999 for a lower figure for support of the Christian Coalition).

Pentecostals and neoevangelicals did not rally to the Moral Majority because of the religious prejudice of its state and local leadership, and it made few inroads among white mainline Protestants, Catholics, or black evangelicals. But the Christian Right groups of the 1990s made a real effort to broaden their coalition, and it appears they may have succeeded. Among movement activists, there is strong evidence that the Christian Right has begun to bridge the religious chasms that so severely limited the potential of the Moral Majority (Wilcox, Rozell, and Gunn, 1996).

Table 5.1 shows the religious identity of Christian Right activists who attended Republican nominating conventions in Virginia in 1993 and 1994 and who attended conventions in Florida, Minnesota, Texas, and Washington in 1995 and

TABLE 5.1

The Christian Right in the States by Religious Identity

	Percent CR/each tradition	Percent each tradition/CR
Virginia		
Mainline	20%	12%
Evangelical	52%	72%
Fundamentalist	43%	82%
Pentecostal	12%	100%
Charismatic	18%	82%
Florida		
Mainline	10%	20%
Evangelical	33%	84%
Fundamentalist	22%	80%
Pentecostal	10%	76%
Charismatic	10%	76%
Minnesota		
Mainline	18%	30%
Evangelical	46%	69%
Fundamentalist	28%	75%
Pentecostal	5%	57%
Charismatic	11%	68%
Texas		
Mainline	20%	12%
Evangelical	52%	72%
Fundamentalist	43%	82%
Pentecostal	12%	100%
Charismatic	18%	82%
Washington		
Mainline	13%	30%
Evangelical	51%	75%
Fundamentalist	39%	80%
Pentecostal	19%	79%
Charismatic	22%	80%

First column is percentage of members of the Christian Right who belong to each religious tradition or who hold each religious identity. Second column shows percentage of those with each religious attribute who are members of the Christian Right.

Source: Surveys conducted of Virginia GOP delegates to 1993 and 1994 nominating conventions and of delegates to other state conventions in 1995–96.

1996. The respondents to this survey were all GOP activists, and thus are not random samples of all Americans. Respondents were permitted to choose more than one religious identity, and many Christian Right activists did so.

The first column shows the distribution of Christian Right members by religious identity; the second column shows the percentage of those with each identity who are members of the Christian Right.[2] For example, the first line of the table shows that 20 percent of Virginia members of the Christian Right identify as mainline Protestants and that 12 percent of those who identify as mainline Protestants in the Virginia Republican party are members of the Christian Right.

The data show that the theological composition of the Christian Right varies by state. The portion who call themselves evangelicals range from a third in Florida to more than half in Virginia, Texas, and Washington. Only 5 percent of Christian Right activists in Minnesota are pentecostal, compared with nearly one in five in Washington state. The data in the second column of the table show that although only a small minority of those who identify as mainline Protestants are members of the Christian Right, large majorities of those who hold other religious identities are members. This confirms that the contemporary Christian Right has indeed bridged theological chasms within American evangelicalism.

Table 5.2 shows the same type of information, this time by denominational affiliation. The Virginia data shows separately evangelical, fundamentalist, and pentecostal denominations, but in the other states these three traditions are combined into a single evangelical category. The data in the first column confirm that the Christian Right in the GOP is dominated by evangelicals, although this does vary by state. In Florida, there are nearly as many mainline Protestant members of Christian Right churches as evangelicals; this may reflect the tendency of most Protestant churches in the South to promote evangelical doctrinal views. In Minnesota nearly a third of members of the Christian Right are Catholics, whereas in Texas that figure is only 7 percent.

The data in the second column show that substantial majorities of those who attend evangelical churches are members of the Christian Right, but that only small minorities of mainline Protestants are members. The percentage of Catholics who are members varies widely by state, ranging from a low of 17 percent in Virginia (where the northern diocese has officially counseled against joining Christian Right groups) to a high of 56 percent in Washington state. In all states except Virginia approximately half of Catholic GOP activists are members of the Christian Right. Of course, only a minority of Catholics are Republicans, so these figures do not suggest that half of all Catholics support the movement (Bendyna, Green, Rozell, and Wilcox, 2000).

●●

TABLE 5.2

The Christian Right in the States by Denomination

	Percent CR/each tradition	Percent each tradition/CR
Virginia		
Mainline Protestant	25%	17%
Evangelical Protestant	29%	55%
Fundamental Protestant	13%	67%
Pentecostal Protestant	13%	80%
Catholic	11%	17%
Florida		
Mainline Protestant	33%	36%
Evangelicals (all)	37%	57%
Catholics	22%	48%
Minnesota		
Mainline Protestant	15%	23%
Evangelicals (all)	52%	67%
Catholics	30%	64%
Texas		
Mainline Protestant	17%	30%
Evangelicals (all)	75%	71%
Catholics	7%	44%
Washington		
Mainline Protestant	14%	24%
Evangelicals (all)	65%	68%
Catholic	14%	56%

Source: Surveys conducted of Virginia GOP delegates to 1993 and 1994 nominating conventions and of delegates to other state conventions in 1995–96.

Thus, the Christian Right is reasonably popular among white evangelicals and has attracted activists among white Catholics and mainline Protestants as well. What are the real limits to its potential expansion? Could the movement capture the support of a majority of Americans? Could it rally black evangelicals to its cause?

In part, the answers to these questions depend on whether pragmatists or ideologues come to dominate the Christian Right. Should pragmatic elements succeed in promoting a moderate agenda, they might be able to rally significant numbers of Americans to their cause. Should the more ideological elements prevail, few outside of the core constituency of the Christian Right will be attracted to the movement.

The best way to demonstrate this point is to examine support for key elements of the Christian Right agenda among various religious constituencies. To illustrate, I have chosen three issues: abortion, gays in the military, and prayer in public schools. Table 5.3 shows the support for various combinations of positions on these issues in 1996. The "extreme" package of positions is strong opposition to gays in the military, opposition to all abortions, and support for spoken general school prayer. Although this set of positions would be popular among movement activists, only a tiny minority of the Christian Right's target constituents hold all three positions. A far larger number hold an extreme position on at least one of the three issues—in most cases, strong opposition to gays in the military. The second issue package is similar to the first but allows for abortion in cases of rape, incest, and danger to the health of the mother. This more moderate position on abortion increases the support for the agenda markedly, but only a small minority supports all three conservative positions.

The third package is more moderate: opposition (strong or weak) to gays in the military, support for at least some restrictions on abortion, and support for spoken prayer in schools. This increases support for the package slightly among all groups. Finally, an even more moderate package includes any opposition to gays in the military, support for any restrictions on abortion, and support for a moment of silence or prayer in public schools. A sizable minority supports all three positions, and an overwhelming majority supports at least one.

Taken together, these data indicate there would be considerable support for a Christian Right that takes moderate positions on most issues and has no single "litmus test"—that is, a movement in which anyone who supports any part of the Christian Right agenda is welcome. There is very little support, however, for the combined package of three extreme positions taken by ideological elements of the movement.

Of course, not all potential members of social movements pay close attention to the nuances of the issue positions of such movements. Scholars have shown that many citizens evaluate social groups based on their relations with other groups and not on the details of their agenda (Sniderman, Brody, and Tetlock, 1991). Thus, white evangelicals and others may evaluate the Christian Coalition as a group that represents conservative Christians and is opposed by feminist, gay rights, secular, and other liberal groups. They may know little about the specific

TABLE 5.3

Support for Christian Right Agenda Under Three Scenarios

| | Evangelicals | | Mainline | |
	White	Black	Protestants	Catholics
Extreme—all 3	3%	1%	0%	2%
—any 1	58%	48%	43%	46%
Extreme with exceptions on abortion				
—all 3	8%	3%	3%	5%
—any 1	75%	60%	58%	64%
Moderate—all 3	12%	6%	6%	7%
—any 1	84%	70%	71%	74%
Moderate with moment silence				
—all 3	33%	13%	16%	15%
—any 1	95%	89%	92%	89%
Consistent Conservatives	28%	6%	15%	14%
Social Conservatives	28%	18%	14%	18%
Total	56%	24%	29%	32%

Source: 1996 National Election Survey.

positions of the organization beyond the impression that it takes conservative stands on social and moral issues.

This suggests that a different way to evaluate the potential constituency for the Christian Right is to use the broad issue groupings discussed in chapter 2. That analysis identified two sets of citizens who were likely supporters of the Christian Right—*consistent conservatives* and *social conservatives.* Table 5.4 shows the distribution of these potential supporters by religious group. More than half of white evangelicals, nearly a third of white Catholics, less than a third of white mainline Protestants, and a quarter of black evangelicals could become supporters of the

TABLE 5.4

Potential Support for the Christian Right (percent)

	Evangelicals		Mainline	
	White (N = 470)	Black (N = 210)	Protestants (N = 401)	Catholics (N = 547)
Consistent conservatives	27	7	16	12
Social conservatives	29	18	13	19
Total	56	25	29	31

Source: 1996 American National Election Survey, 1992.

movement if it limits its agenda to social issues and values and adopts mostly moderate issue positions.

Should the Christian Right succeed in appealing to these potential constituents, it would have the backing of nearly a quarter of the American citizenry. Although this would be far short of a real "moral majority," it would represent a sizable movement, substantially larger than the feminist or civil rights movements of the 1960s and 1970s. Moreover, if a majority of these activists worked solely within the Republican party, they could exert control over party nominations and platforms. Finally, it is important to remember that the Christian Right's political influence extends beyond its membership, for voter guides distributed by sympathetic church members or pastors can influence the votes of those who are not members of the movement and even of those who are not supporters.

The data also suggest that the Christian Right may be reaching its maximum level of support among white evangelicals. Indeed, the 56 percent of white evangelicals who belong to the two sympathetic issue groupings exactly matches the 56 percent that polls show currently support the Christian Right. Although the Christian Right can presumably continue to expand its activist base among supporters in this constituency, there are substantial limits to appealing to the remaining white evangelicals, because many are liberal on social issues.

Of course, no social movement reaches its entire potential audience. There are barriers to mobilizing conservative Catholics, different barriers to enlisting white mainline Protestants, and very different barriers to mobilizing black evangelicals. Different strategies might be needed for each target audience. The Christian Right faces internal dilemmas in choosing its strategies. And Christian conservatives face a dilemma as well.

Dilemma 1: Moderation in the Defense of Virtue?

The data in table 5.3 suggest that the movement can attract its largest possible constituency by staking moderate positions on most issues. The Christian Coalition attempted to do that, focusing its agenda on pragmatic issues where there is some public support. Instead of seeking to ban all abortions, the Coalition in 1999 sought legislation banning the transportation of teenaged girls across state lines for abortions and bans on "partial birth" abortions. Instead of focusing exclusively on the social issue concerns of its members, the coalition backed the agenda of economic conservatives, including support for a flat tax and privatization of the welfare system and pushing in 1999 for an end to the "marriage penalty" of the federal tax code. The strategy of the Christian Coalition is to adopt a moderate face, to compromise on key issues to achieve some change in policy, and to cooperate with other elements of the Republican party to win their support for portions of the Christian Right agenda.

The Christian Coalition's strategy has the potential to appeal to many Americans. Although few favor banning abortions, many support some restrictions and a sizable number support a ban on "partial-birth" abortions. Most social movements have spawned at least one large national organization that made moderate, mainstream appeals—the NAACP and NOW are but two examples—and these organizations serve to attract support from a wide audience. It is possible that the Christian Coalition will become the NAACP of the Christian Right. Yet the organizational troubles of the Christian Coalition also create the possibility that the movement will solidify without a large moderate group.

Although the moderate approach has the advantage of broad appeal, moderation does not inspire activists to devote their evenings to the cause. Many activists have left the organization over Pat Robertson's call for moderation on abortion and his advice to abandon the effort to impeach the president. The loud applause at the 1999 Christian Coalition convention for speakers who took strong positions on abortion and defense suggests that the activists of the movement are not entirely happy with moderation.

The danger of the moderate strategy is that the movement may win a larger audience but lose one of its key assets—the enthusiasm of its volunteers. Activism is not common in America, and most citizens can find more enjoyable things to do after a hard day at work or with their children than stuffing envelopes or working fax machines. Many Christian Right activists see themselves battling for the soul of America, but they may be less willing to engage in combat for goals that they perceive as involving too much compromise.

Many activists argue that it is better to "fight a good fight" than to compromise with the world.[3] They favor banning late-term abortions but think that this would be only a tiny victory and prefer that the movement work publicly to ban all abortions. They seek a spoken school prayer rather than a moment of silence when students might pass notes or plan their after-school activities. They want to enforce laws against homosexuality rather than merely keep gays and lesbians from adopting children.

An examination of Christian Right direct-mail appeals shows that the financial constituency of the movement prefers the strategy of ideological purity. One fundraising professional who has mailed to Christian Right lists on behalf of conservative presidential candidates told me that the only way to raise money from these activists is to promise to pursue vigorously an uncompromising ideological agenda.

The solution to this dilemma for the Christian Right may be specialization. While the Christian Coalition attempts to bargain with moderate Republicans and attract a broad audience, the Family Research Council can take a more conservative stance. A spate of groups that specialize in certain issues (such as Citizens for Excellence in Education) can make extreme rhetorical appeals and take highly ideological positions and thereby maintain morale among the activists.

Dilemma 2: The Republican Big Tent

The second dilemma for the Christian Right is whether to concentrate its efforts solely within the Republican party, pursue a more nonpartisan stance, or form a third party. Currently the movement is concentrated almost solely in the Republican party and controls many state party organizations. The parade of presidential hopefuls at the Christian Coalition convention in 1999 demonstrated that many expected the Christian Right to play an important role in the 2000 elections and that it would be difficult for a candidate to win the nomination or the general election without the movement's tacit approval.

But the marriage between the Christian Right and the Republican party has not always been a happy one. Many party moderates resent the influence of the Christian Right in candidate selection and in party platforms, and many Christian conservatives resented the efforts by party leaders to engineer the early nomination of George W. Bush for president and the history of party moderates' refusing to endorse Christian conservative candidates who win intraparty struggles. The passionate struggle over the 1996 presidential nomination platform suggests that these two party factions do not always get along.

Between 1980 and 1992, abortion was a litmus-test issue in presidential politics in both parties. In 1998, Jesse Jackson and Richard Gephardt became pro-choice to run for the presidency, and George Bush became pro-life. More recently, many Republicans have argued that the party is a "big tent" with room for pro-choice and pro-life candidates and activists, for moderates and Christian conservatives.

The Christian Coalition appears willing to set up a booth under that big tent and has worked on behalf of moderately pro-choice Republicans against more strongly pro-choice Democrats. But others in the movement point out that the tent has exits, and they indicate they will leave the party rather than support pro-choice candidates. In 1999, Patrick Buchanan bolted the GOP for the Reform party, arguing that the Republicans were indistinguishable from Democrats on most issues. Christian conservative Senator Bob Smith from New Hampshire also briefly left the GOP.

Such uneasy relations between parties and social movements are common. Social movements and parties must negotiate a mutually satisfactory relationship, for the two have different goals and different resources. Social movements have voters, activists, money, and means of mobilizing them. Parties have easy access to the electoral ballot, an even larger set of supporters, and experience in running and winning campaigns. Social movements would like to use the party machinery to elect their candidates and use the party platform to advance their policy goals. Parties would like to use the activists, money, and communication channels of social movements to support their regular candidates.

Indeed, in the early 1990s, feminists and African Americans also threatened to launch independent candidates or start third parties if the Democrats did not accede to their policy demands. In neither case was the threat taken especially seriously, and no one expects the Christian Right to bolt the Republican party.

But there is a growing possibility that this troubled marriage might end in divorce. After five years in control of the Congress, the Republican majority had yet to pass much of the Christian Right's social agenda. The party has provided important policy gestures to other elements of the GOP coalition but has mostly given symbolic victories to the movement. Newt Gingrich, the speaker of the House in 1998, promised Christian Right activists that he would focus on three goals: a ban on partial-birth abortions over the president's veto, elimination of the National Endowment for the Arts, and an end to the marriage penalty in taxes. None of this has happened. Many activists are distinctly unhappy about this, and criticism of the GOP Congress at the 1999 Christian Coalition convention met with loud applause.

If the Christian Right did leave the Republican party, it could choose to work within both parties to influence candidate nominations, or it could pursue a more nonpartisan strategy. Such a course would have the potential to attract a somewhat wider audience, including more conservative Catholics and especially African Americans. The success of the Christian Right in assembling a large coalition in the New York school board races shows the potential of a nonpartisan strategy. Indeed, a bipartisan Christian Right might well have a greater policy impact than the current incarnation focused within the GOP.

Dilemma 3: Do I Stay or Do I Go?

Christian conservatives face a larger dilemma—whether to continue building a social movement that is primarily political, or to concentrate instead on building infrastructure and alternative institutions in their own religious community. In 1999, Paul Weyrich announced that the culture war was lost. "If there really were a moral majority out there, Bill Clinton would have been driven out of office months ago," he said. "It is not only the lack of political will of the Republicans, although that is part of the problem. More powerful is the fact that what Americans found absolutely intolerable only a few years ago, a majority not only tolerates but celebrates." Weyrich argues that the Christian Right's cultural agenda cannot be accomplished through politics and counsels instead that Christian conservatives withdraw from the culture and build alternative institutions to promote and protect their values.

Former Moral Majority activists Cal Thomas and Ed Dobson in 1999 produced a book that argues that Christian conservatives became obsessed with political victory, and in the process abandoned some of their core principles (Thomas and Dobson, 1999). They suggest that the Christians should not withdraw entirely from politics but that they should focus on their primary goals of winning souls for Christ and of changing the culture through persuasion.

If Christian conservatives abandon the Christian Right early in the new millennium, it might appear to signal the end of the latest wave of the movement. If past experience is any guide, however, evangelicals would continue to build alternative institutions and infrastructure. Moreover, the movement could possibly emerge stronger if it engages the culture more broadly and is not so strongly tied to any one party.

What Thomas and Weyrich are suggesting is that evangelicals begin to persuade the public of the validity of their positions, using reason and not political power. Thus conservative Christians could attempt to persuade citizens that abortion is the wrong choice, that the homosexual lifestyle is sinful but can be abandoned, or that families are happier if the mother stays home with the children.

Many Christian Right activists strongly object to Weyrich's and Thomas's call to withdraw from partisan politics, however. They see the possibility in 2001 of having a Republican president and a GOP Congress. In many states such as Virginia, the GOP may well control the legislature in 2001 and the voters of the state may elect a movement figure as governor. This suggests a broader question: could the Christian Right win?

Can the Christian Right Come to Power?

Those who most fear the Christian Right wonder if its elites could ever seize power and control American politics, perhaps someday ruling by force as the Nazis did in Germany. Such fears are almost certainly unfounded. Most leaders of the Christian Right are committed to the democratic process and strongly supportive of the American political system (Lienesch, 1994; Reed, 1994a). Although some Christian Right activists would like to restrict the civil liberties of their political opponents, only a few isolated extremists would abolish elections and seek to rule by force.[4]

Others worry that Christian Right activists might win control of the Republican party and perhaps gain control of the political system through democratic means and enact their entire policy agenda. This is also unlikely. The American political system was designed specifically to prevent any single faction from dominating politics. The shared powers of the presidency, the Congress, and the U.S. Supreme Court provide many avenues to thwart the policy program of any one political group. Even if a Christian Right candidate were someday to win the presidency and the Republicans were to retain control of Congress, there would be internal fighting within the party in Congress, the Supreme Court could overturn laws, and state and local governments would retain the authority to legislate policy on education, gay rights, and abortion. The American system would prevent any organized group from imposing its will on a majority opposed to its agenda.

This means that liberals' worst nightmares of an American theocracy are probably just nightmares. But it does not mean that the Christian Right cannot affect public policy in the United States. Consider the profound changes to policy and government brought about by the civil rights and feminist movements in a relatively short period. In the early 1960s, blacks could not vote in many southern counties, eat in many restaurants, swim in many swimming pools, or stay in many hotels. There were separate drinking fountains for blacks and whites, and a black section in the back of the bus. Today racism persists, but racial discrimination by businesses is greatly diminished, and blacks have won elected offices from county boards to city mayors to the governorship.

Similarly, the feminist movement of the 1960s and 1970s radically altered social relations in the United States. Although women remain disadvantaged in many aspects of society, they now constitute more than half of the graduating classes in major law schools and have achieved positions of power in politics, business, and society. Sexism, like racism, persists in society, but women have many more life choices today than in the 1950s.

To evaluate the impact of the civil rights, feminist, and Christian Right movement, imagine that Rip Van Winkle had fallen asleep during the GOP nominating convention of 1960 and wakened during the 1996 convention. He would not have been surprised by the conservative Christian rhetoric—indeed he would have been somewhat surprised to hear some Republicans speak openly of supporting abortion rights. He would have been quite startled, however, to watch the moderate GOP delegates enthusiastically welcoming an African-American military leader, Colin Powell, and later that week to see the social conservatives responding with equal fervor to a black congressman, J. C. Watts. And he would have been very surprised to see the keynote address given by a woman who served in the House of Representatives, while her husband held their child on his lap in the audience. Clearly, the civil rights and feminist movements have transformed society in a much more profound way than the Christian Right.

To determine whether the Christian Right could possibly have such a great impact on American society, it is first necessary to consider just what the movement has accomplished to date. There has been continuous Christian Right activity in the United States for more than twenty years, and it is useful to assess just how successful these efforts have been.

On the core issues of the Christian Right agenda, there has been only marginal success. States are now free to impose procedural restrictions on access to abortions, such as requiring teenagers to notify their parents and women to wait twenty-four hours before obtaining an abortion. Although some states have made abortion more difficult to obtain, many have not. Moreover, even where access to abortion has been made more difficult, ultimately any adult woman who is determined to obtain an abortion and has the resources to travel to places where abortions are performed may still do so. These restrictions strike pro-choice Americans as an intolerable infringement on their reproductive liberties, but America is far from the ban on all abortions that most Christian Right activists seek.

Gays and lesbians are also more integrated into American public life and protected from discrimination. Many large companies now offer benefits to the partners of gay employees, and several television shows and movies have depicted gay
and lesbian characters in positive or sympathetic light. In 2000, Vermont created a
legal partnership for gay or lesbian couples. A political scientist, Craig Rimmerman, observed in 1995:

> The gay and lesbian movement has achieved a number of victories at all levels of gov-
> ernment. Undoubtedly, it is easier for someone to be openly gay or lesbian now than
> it was in the United States at the end of the 1970s. There are many more openly gay
> and lesbian role models in all walks of life. But there is much more to be done in
> terms of prompting government policymakers at all levels to create public policy that
> protects the rights of gays and lesbians to live their lives free from open discrimina-
> tion and prejudice.[5]

Prayer is still barred from public schools, although high school administrators
are increasingly aware that this does not prohibit students from offering a quiet
personal prayer before lunch or reading their Bibles in study hall. Public school
curricula remain secular, and evolution is taught in biology classes across the
country. Sex education is taught in most communities, and although that curriculum generally encourages abstinence, it also teaches sexually active teenagers
how to minimize their chances of disease or pregnancy.

Moreover, after twenty years of preaching in the wilderness, the Christian Right
has not persuaded Americans of the wisdom of its policies. Indeed, if anything
there have been small but significant trends toward greater liberalism on most of
the key issues of concern to the Christian Right, especially on gay rights. Figure 5.1
shows the percentage of Americans who approve of Supreme Court decisions to
bar prayer and Bible readings from classrooms, who oppose any restrictions on
abortion and on pornography for adults, and who believe that homosexual relations are always acceptable. The data begin in 1978, the year of the foundation of
Moral Majority and Christian Voice, and show increased liberalism on gay rights
and little change on abortion, pornography, or school prayer. It is unlikely that the
public will become more conservative on these issues in the future, for the
youngest Americans are far more liberal than the oldest cohorts they are replacing.

The concentrated efforts of the Christian Right to overturn restrictions on religious practice have had some real success, and it is on this issue that the movement is most likely to make real gains in the future. In 1994 President Clinton
spoke of the need to allow religious expression in the public schools, and as a result of lobbying by the Christian Right and the threat of lawsuits from the move-

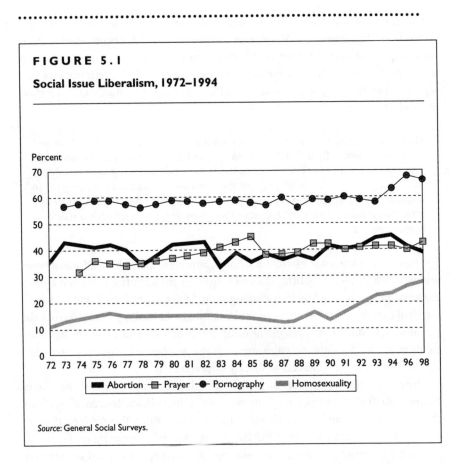

FIGURE 5.1

Social Issue Liberalism, 1972–1994

Source: General Social Surveys.

ment's legal arm, many communities and school districts have become more accommodating to religious expression by conservative Christians.

At the state and local level, Christian Right activity has had a greater impact on public policy. This is perhaps most apparent in the field of education; various curricula and programs have been dropped because of organized protests by parents, including the teaching of modern scientific thinking in biology, geology, and astronomy. In some cities, gay rights laws have been overturned, and abortion is more difficult to obtain today in many states than it was in 1978.

Perhaps more important is the impact the Christian Right has had in framing the policy agenda, as noted by political scientist Kenneth Wald:

It is difficult to identify any substantive public policy that has been implemented primarily because of the Christian Right. Rather, the mobilization of conservative Christians has affected the agenda of American politics, promoting some issues from obscurity to a central place on the national agenda. We would probably not be arguing about school prayer, tuition vouchers, and other proposals had the Christian Right failed to materialize.[6]

Of course, Christian Right activists seek to do more than affect the policy debate—they wish to alter public policy, to change the direction of America, and to redeem it from what they see as its sinful path. Whether they can accomplish any of this remains to be seen.

What are the prospects for Christian Right success in its policy agenda?. Its peripheral economic agenda is perhaps most likely to be enacted, since it has the support of economic conservatives in the Republican party. It is also possible that the Christian Right can win some fights that relate to its core agenda: banning pornography from the Internet, banning the transportation of girls across state lines to obtain abortions, and passing parental notification bills in more states.

The Christian Right's efforts to provide greater accommodation for religion in public life are perhaps the most popular aspect of its agenda. Clear majorities of Americans favor a moment of silence in public schools, prayers at high school sporting events and graduation ceremonies, and other public displays of Christianity. On religious matters, the greatest barrier for the Christian Right is structural: The U.S. Supreme Court decides church-state issues, and although the court has been far more accepting of religious accommodation in recent years, it is unlikely to approve of all of the policies the Christian Right proposes. Thus, the only way to realize these policies is to amend the Constitution or to change radically the composition of the Supreme Court.

The proposed Religious Freedom Amendment to the U.S. Constitution faces the hurdles designed by the founding fathers to make the Constitution difficult to change. The failure of popular amendments such as the ERA and the amendment to ban the burning of the U.S. flag, is clear evidence that momentary passions are not enough to change the Constitution. Moreover, the concentrated opposition by many mainstream Christian and Jewish groups makes the prospects for the amendment at best a long shot.

The odds are even longer for many of the other policies of the Christian Right. Some important demographic trends suggest that America is unlikely to ban abortions, to begin to enforce sodomy laws, or to adopt laws making it more difficult for women to work outside the home. First, generational replacement is producing a nation that is more tolerant of different lifestyles and more supportive of individual freedoms. On most of the key items on the Christian Right agenda, the generation most supportive of Christian Right positions is the oldest one, which is gradually being replaced by younger citizens who are far more liberal (Cook, Jelen, and Wilcox, 1993). Although the youngest Americans are somewhat more conservative than those who grew up during the 1960s, they are far more liberal on abortion, sexual morality, and other lifestyle issues than their grandparents.

Second, America is becoming a better-educated country, and those Americans who have completed a college degree are the most liberal on these issues as well. This does not mean that Christian Right activists are poorly educated or that all college graduates are cultural liberals, but those who have completed college are far more liberal on abortion and gay rights than those whose formal education ended with high school. For a variety of reasons, a college education seems to lead to support for individual liberties and a greater tolerance for those who choose different lifestyles (Cook, Jelen, and Wilcox, 1992).

Overall, then, it appears likely that the Christian Right will affect policy only at the margins. It will ultimately succeed primarily in helping the economic conservatives of the Republican party achieve their agenda and in eliminating whatever real discrimination exists against conservative Christians. Why should such a large social movement fail to work its will, when the civil rights and feminist movements have had such a large impact on American life?

Each of these more successful movements had as its primary goal the amelioration of real social and economic discrimination against its movement constituency. Blacks and women were denied jobs, promotions, housing, credit, and access to political office. Such discrimination clearly ran against American notions of fairness and equal opportunity, and the movements ultimately have helped reduce this discrimination.

Although the Christian Right claims that evangelicals face real discrimination, at best they face cultural, not economic, bias. Christians are not being denied jobs, promotions, housing, credit, or the chance to run for higher office. Moreover, despite the heated rhetoric of Christian Right direct mail, conservative Christians are free to worship in America as they choose and are in no danger of losing that right. In a country that is overwhelmingly Christian, many Americans regard claims that Christians face serious bias as unbelievable.

The Christian Right has been successful when it has pointed to real discrimination in America. Some misguided school principals have interfered with student religious freedom because they misinterpreted Supreme Court rulings, and the movement has made great strides in protecting student rights. The recent U.S. Supreme Court ruling that the University of Virginia should provide funds to student religious publications if it funds other kinds of student publications is a case in point. The Christian Right has also been somewhat successful in its advocacy for a greater public acknowledgment of religion in America.

The Christian Right has also succeeded in playing the role of the "Christian Anti-Defamation League," responding quickly and forcefully to real and perceived slights in the media and public life. For example, in December 1995 a poet who regularly contributed to National Public Radio was forced to apologize for comments after Ralph Reed quickly denounced his remarks. Just as the civil rights movement succeeded in making racist jokes unacceptable in polite company and the feminist movement banished sexist and off-color jokes, so the Christian Right seeks to bar demeaning humor aimed at conservative Christians.

At some point evangelicals may succeed in making the point that popular culture has few positive depictions of the lifestyles of a quarter of the American public. In 1999 black Americans justifiably protested the heavily white fall lineup on the major television networks, but evangelical Christians were far more underrepresented. Television in recent years has featured a few angels and some characters who took religion seriously, but sympathetic portraits of born-again Christians are non-existent.

In all of these areas, the Christian Right has had some success and will probably continue to do so in the future. But the core of the Christian Right agenda is not just about allowing conservative Christians to practice their religion and avoid public ridicule; it is about legislating morality. The Christian Right seeks to legislate policies that affect the behavior of others—their sexual relationships, their access to abortion, their ability to read what they choose. Because these behaviors lie in what some have called the "sphere of privacy," social change is much more difficult to achieve. Blacks and women were able to achieve much by calling on Americans to confront their own discriminatory behavior. The Christian Right asks people not just to stop discriminating against Christians but to live their lives according to its version of morality and religion. This is a much harder sell.

Premillennialists in the New Millennium

In 2000 the Christian Right stands at the crossroads. Its future is far murkier than when I wrote the first edition of this book five years ago. It is possible that the Christian Right will continue to institutionalize, that the Christian Coalition will rebuild its organization, and that the movement will continue to recruit young, talented leaders committed to the long haul who will not go gently into that good night in response to temporary setbacks. It is also possible that the movement will fragment, with some following Pat Buchanan and others out of the GOP, others remaining as part of the Republican coalition, and still others withdrawing from politics altogether to build alternative institutions. The 2000 elections will be critical to the future of the movement.

In part, the future of the movement depends on whether pragmatists or ideologues dominate the movement. If the ideological wing of the Christian Right comes to dominate the movement, leading it to take relatively extreme positions with little room for compromise, the Christian Right probably will continue for a time to have a strong core of activists. Relations between the movement and Republican party regulars will remain strained, for candidates who adopt the positions of the ideological wing of the movement generally lose general elections. Moderate Republicans outnumber ideological Christian Right activists, so eventually the moderate wing of the party will win. Disheartened by its inability to control party nominations or platforms, the Christian Right may offer some independent candidates, but the movement will probably fade away.

It is also possible, however, that the pragmatic wing of the movement will dominate, and the Christian Right will develop into a major faction in the Republican party and a set of significant interest groups. Like other party factions, it will offer candidates for public office who will sometimes win; like other interest groups, it will press its demands on governments and will sometimes succeed. The social movement will solidify into more permanent organizations that must bargain with others at the pluralist table of American politics.

If the Christian Right moderates win, it is likely that the activist core of the movement will become even more disenchanted with politics. Some activists will tire of laboring in the political vineyards for little reward and will leave politics altogether. Others will remain active and become socialized into the norms of bargaining and compromise. If the Christian Right is to become an active part of American pluralism, its leadership will need to facilitate that socialization process, and this means reducing perceptions of threat that drive the intolerance of movement activists.

Political scientist John Green has offered this prediction:

> The long march of the Christian Right from inchoate movement to sophisticated political force is not yet over. The movement is likely to continue to expand and consolidate its gains through the arrival of the millennium, reaching its natural limits soon after. At that point it will face a real dilemma: institutionalize or become irrelevant. In either case, the Christian Right as a movement will begin to fade. How this crucial turning point is handled will determine what legacy the movement leaves in national politics and policy.[7]

Such ultimately is the fate of most social movements. The energies of the civil rights and feminist movements have generally ebbed, although both have spawned potent factions in the Democratic party and important and skilled interest groups.

Ted Jelen (1990) has argued that support for the Christian Right waxes and wanes in a cyclical fashion. As cultural minorities become visible and make demands for social justice, Christian Right movements arise to enforce conventional morality. Yet the movements inevitably fail because of the religious prejudice of the various elements of the movement, and religion again becomes a private matter. Jelen's account seems to fit nicely the rise and fall of the fundamentalist movements of the 1920s, 1950s, and 1980s, but if the movement collapses again it will not be from religious particularism but instead from the failure of the electoral strategy to lead to the movement's policy goals. Most likely, the Christian Right will probably become institutionalized as a permanent fixture in American politics—a significant collection of interest groups and national, state, and local party factions.

Conclusion

In this book I have explored two radically divergent visions of the Christian Right: In the first it is an intolerant, uncompromising movement that would deprive women, gays and lesbians, and others of their rights; in the second it is a defensive movement that would protect conservative Christians from a hostile society and government. As in most heated political debates, the truth appears to lie somewhere in between these two positions. Ultimately the Christian Right probably poses only a limited threat to basic American civil liberties because it is unlikely to gain access to sufficient political power to enact legislation and because many activists hold conflicting values of intolerance and democratic government. And although the agenda of the Christian Right is in some ways defensive, the movement also asks Americans to adopt policies that would affect the lives and liberties of many citizens.

Is the movement good or bad for America? The answer for each person depends partially on the individual's reactions to the agenda of the Christian Right. For someone who supports sharp restrictions on abortion and on civil rights protections for gays and lesbians and who supports the teaching of creationism and school prayer, the Christian Right appears to be a very good thing. For someone who opposes those policies, the movement appears to be a threatening, hostile force.

It is important to go beyond these political calculations, however, and assess the positive and negative things the movement has accomplished. Because these judgments are ultimately normative, I conclude with my personal evaluation of the movement. I write as someone who opposes most of the policy goals of the Christian Right but who supports the free exercise of religion for conservative Christians and all other Americans and believes that Christian conservatives deserve a place in the political process.

There are several positive aspects to the involvement of the Christian Right in American politics. The mobilization of previously apolitical evangelicals and fundamentalists into politics constitutes a useful broadening of the electorate and of the active public. America's pluralist system works best when all important groups are represented in policy negotiations, and the Christian Right's constituency has a unique set of policy concerns that should be part of the policy debate.

The careful monitoring of the rights of religious expression in public schools has also been a positive result, for in a few communities Christian children have been prohibited from engaging in religious activities that do not disrupt the school curriculum. Moreover, the efforts by the Christian Right to counter negative stereotypes in news and popular media have been generally helpful, although claims that anyone who opposes the movement exhibits anti-Christian bias are disingenuous.

Probably the most important benefit of the Christian Right has been its insistence that America consider basic moral and religious values as it crafts public policy. Often policy debates in America are artificially devoid of any discussion of values, and the Christian Right deserves some credit for the rediscovery of their importance in the 1990s. Moreover, because many Americans are deeply religious, it is odd to deny the role of religious values in policy debates, and the Christian Right has gone far toward legitimizing the inclusion of these values in the larger discussion of America's agenda. If the Christian Right forces America to consider its core values and to connect those values to public policy, it will have been a positive force.

The values the Christian Right brings to the debate are but one set of religious values, of course, and I hope that others will engage movement participants in a discussion of competing values, such as social justice, equality, and personal liberation. A political scientist, Clarke Cochran, responded to a paper by Ralph Reed at a conference in the 1990s by noting: "A lot of issues that Christians should be supporting, such things as gun control, justice in health care, protecting the vulnerable widows and orphans (to use Biblical language), dignified work for people, and property for the common good (from the Catholic natural law tradition) never appear because . . . the Christian Coalition. . . has been captured by the conservative ideological position."[8] Cochran's analysis is but one example of the useful debate that could be undertaken on the religious values that underlie public policy.

Yet I also see some negative aspects to Christian Right involvement in American politics. The harsh, uncompromising moral certitude of many Christian Right activists often does not further the policy debate but rather precludes it. For many activists, there is no room for debate, because they see their policy preferences as the will of God. One activist in Virginia told me in no uncertain terms that a flat tax was biblical policy, and therefore there was no room for discussion. Such certitude actually discourages the inclusion of religious values in the policy debate, for it brands alternative values as illegitimate and encourages others to steer clear of religious argument.

The heated rhetoric of Christian Right direct mail exacerbates this problem by telling contributors that an alliance of liberal groups may take over America, strip them of their basic religious rights, teach their children Satan worship and witchcraft, and implement other almost unspeakably evil policies. It is small wonder that many Christian Right activists fear their political enemies and consider them a danger to the republic. Liberal groups also contribute to this climate of cultural conflict by portraying conservative Christians as jack-booted thugs who would overturn American democracy. The tone of political discourse would be improved if both sides would calm down a bit.

Moreover, the failure of many Christian Right activists to support basic civil liberties is troubling. When movement leaders write that gays and lesbians, feminists, liberals, and secular citizens should not be permitted to teach in schools, they invite their followers to take action against teachers in school districts across the country. At the fringe of the movement, some write that America has no room for anyone but Christian conservatives.

The lasting legacy of the Christian Right will depend critically on whether pragmatists or ideologues come to dominate the movement, on how those new leaders choose to mold the movement, and on the willingness of their followers to be so molded. If pragmatic leaders dominate, counsel the virtues of bargaining and compromise, and encourage their activists to think of their political antagonists as reasonable citizens with basic rights, the movement may ultimately prove to be a constructive voice in the policy debate. If ideological leaders warn darkly of the dangers of the forces of liberalism and stir up hatred toward gays and lesbians, feminists, secularists, and others with whom they do not agree, the movement will constitute a divisive force in America that threatens the lifestyles of many citizens.

If Christian conservatives choose to follow the suggestion of Cal Thomas and Ed Dobson to pull back from partisan political action and to instead engage the culture in a debate and discussion of the religious and moral underpinnings of public policy, it is possible that the movement will have its greatest, and most positive, impact. Because of the partisan nature of the current incarnation of the movement, there has been more shouting than discussion, and both sides have ended up adopting more extreme positions in an effort to mobilize voters. Between the shouting voices there is room for a quieter discussion, where both sides might be surprised that they have some common ground.

Discussion Questions

Chapter 1

1. How do terms such as "Christian Right," "religious Right," "pro-family movement," and "Christian conservative" differ in their meaning? What are the advantages and disadvantages of each term?

2. What is a social movement? How does this label fit the Christian Right? What are examples of other social movements?

3. Why is the Christian Right controversial?

4. How doe American religious diversity, civil religion, and constitutional context affect your assessment of the Christian Right?

Chapter 2

1. What have been the common themes of different waves of Christian Right activity? How have these various manifestations of the Christian Right differed?

2. Why do fundamentalists object to teaching evolution in public schools? Do parents have a right to see that their children are exposed only to ideas of which they approve, or does society have the right to expose children to different ideas as part of the educational process?

3. How do fundamentalists, evangelicals, pentecostals, and charismatics differ? Why are these differences important to individuals within these traditions?

Chapter 3

1. Consider two theses: (a) The various groups of the contemporary Christian Right compete with one another for members, confuse their constituency by taking different policy positions, and foster rivalries. They constitute a weakness for the movement. (b) The various groups of the contemporary Christian Right are an advantage to the movement because they allow activists to choose among several groups based on their issue positions and emphasis and thereby attract a wider audience. Which thesis do you think is true and why?

2. In the 1980s nearly all media attention went to the Moral Majority, and during the 1990s nearly all attention was focused on the Christian Coalition. Why?

3. Some writers classify the pro-life movement as part of the Christian Right, but this book does not. What are the arguments for making each designation?

4. How does the Christian Right seek to influence government? How do these strategies and tactics differ from those of the civil rights movement or the feminist movement?

5. What are the advantages and disadvantages to the Republican party that result from its alliance with the Christian Right? What are the advantages and disadvantages to the Christian Right from this alliance?

Chapter 4

1. Why might mobilizing evangelicals and other conservative Christians into politics provide a more balanced policy debate?

2. Why do you think Christian Right activists are less supportive than other activists of basic civil liberties? Does this lack of support pose a danger to democracy? How might Christian Right leaders help to increase support for civil liberties among their activist core?

3. Consider the policy agenda of the Christian Right. Why do Christian Right supporters believe that theirs is a defensive agenda, and why do the movement's opponents think that it is an offensive agenda?

4. Is the Christian Right good or bad for America? Does the movement enhance democracy by mobilizing a new group into the policy debate, or does it threaten democracy and civil liberties?

Chapter 5

1. Will the Christian Right be able to expand its base among white evangelicals? What are its prospects for attracting Catholics, mainline Protestants, and African Americans?

2. What are the advantages and disadvantages to a strategy of moderation by the Christian Right? What would the movement gain and what would it lose by adopting this strategy?

3. In what ways has the Christian Right affected public policy in America? In what ways has it changed the terms of the debate?

4. Is the Christian Right good or bad for America? Why?

Glossary

Accommodationist Person who believes that the First Amendment permits the government to support all religions so long as it does not discriminate among religions. Accommodationists welcome public displays of religious symbols and practice.

American Center for Law and Justice Legal organization of the contemporary Christian Right, associated with Pat Robertson and spearheaded by Jay Sekulow. The ACLJ files lawsuits on behalf of Christians who believe they have faced discrimination.

American Civil Liberties Union Organization devoted to protecting First Amendment liberties for all Americans, usually through legal action. The group has defended religious liberties of unpopular groups and sought to maintain a strong separation between church and state.

American Council of Christian Churches Militant fundamentalist organization, formed in 1941 by Carl McIntyre. The ACCC denounced communist infiltration in society and in mainline Protestant churches and provided resources to the anticommunist groups of the 1950s.

American Family Association Organization of the contemporary Christian Right, originally known as the National Federation for Decency, headed by Donald Wildmon. The AFA focuses primarily on monitoring sex and violence on television and on countering anti-Christian stereotypes on television. It organizes consumer boycotts of the sponsors of offending programs.

Bible Crusaders of America Antievolution organization of the 1920s. The BCA was well funded, linked to Baptist churches, and active primarily in the South.

Bible League of North America Organization formed in 1902 that, through arguments and publications, fought the teaching of evolution.

Born-again experience Experience common in evangelical churches in which an individual repents of his or her sin, accepts Christ as his or her personal savior, and is redeemed by grace. Often an emotional experience, accompanied by a sense of release.

Catholic Alliance Organization launched in 1995 by the Christian Coalition to attract Catholic support for the Christian Right.

Charismatic Term used to refer to a religious movement and to certain religious doctrines. Charismatics worship with ecstatic spiritual gifts, including speaking in tongues, faith healing, and being slain in the Spirit. The charismatic movement transcends denominational boundaries, with charismatic caucuses in most denominations and interfaith charismatic gatherings in most major cities.

Christian Anti-Communism Crusade Anticommunist organization of the 1950s, which used radio and traveling schools of anticommunism to spread its message. The CACC exists today.

Christian Coalition   Organization of the contemporary Christian Right, headed by Pat Robertson. The Christian Coalition is the largest extant group and is generally more moderate than other organizations.

Christian Crusade   Anticommunist organization of the 1950s.

Christian preferentialist   Individual who takes an accommodationist position on the establishment clause of the First Amendment and a communitarian position on the free exercise clause. A Christian preferentialist seeks a more open display of Christian symbols and faith but is less willing to allow displays of other American religions.

Christian reconstructionism   Also known as dominion theology and theonomy, this doctrine teaches that American law and politics should be structured along the lines of Old Testament law.

Christian Voice   Christian Right organization founded in the late 1970s by Robert Grant with the help of Pat Robertson. The Christian Voice was known for its lobbying and ridiculed for its voters guides, which nonetheless served as the precursors for more sophisticated contemporary efforts. The organization exists today.

Church League of America   Anticommunist organization of the 1950s.

Citizens for Excellence in Education   Organization of the contemporary Christian Right, headed by Robert Simonds. CEE opposes the teaching of secular humanism and witchcraft in schools and opposes programs to establish national education standards, such as outcomes-based education.

Civil religion   A set of beliefs about the relationship between God and country, generally centering on a special relationship. In America, civil religion is evident in the frequent references to religious images in public life.

Communitarian (First Amendment)   View that religious liberties can be limited by community norms. Communitarians generally disapprove of religious exemptions from otherwise valid laws and hold that the free exercise clause bars government from directly prohibiting religious observance but not from limiting such observance if the law has a secular purpose.

Concerned Maine Families   Organization of the contemporary Christian Right that sought to pass a referendum in Maine in 1995 that would have barred local jurisdictions from passing laws forbidding job discrimination against gays and lesbians.

Concerned Women for America   Organization of the contemporary Christian Right, headed by Beverly LaHaye. CWA is composed primarily of women and takes a special interest in women's issues.

Contract with the American Family   Political document by the Christian Coalition that includes ten policy goals.

Creationism   The belief that the world, its flora and fauna, were created by God and that he made humans at that time. Creationists explicitly reject the theory of evolution. Most believe that the world was created in six days in the relatively recent past.

Defenders of the Christian Faith   Antievolution organization of the 1920s, active primarily in the Midwest.

Dispensationalism Doctrine that God has dealt with humans under different covenants or dispensations at different times in history. Although accounts vary, many dispensationalists believe that the first covenant was the period of innocence in the Garden of Eden, which ended with Eve and the apple; the second was mankind on its own, which ended with the flood of Noah; the third was chastened humanity, which ended with the Tower of Babel; the fourth was God's promise to Abraham, which ended with the captivity in Egypt; the fifth was the covenant with Moses; the sixth was the period of grace ushered in by Jesus; and the seventh will be the millennium, a thousand-year period of perfect peace.

Eagle Forum Antifeminist organization headed by Phyllis Schlafly. Eagle Forum was organized to fight the Equal Rights Amendment in the 1970s and now focuses on opposition to feminism, to the teaching of secular humanism, and to legal abortion.

Establishment clause Phrase in the First Amendment that is source of controversy regarding separation of church and state: "Congress shall make no law respecting an establishment of religion."

Evangelical Term used to refer to a religious movement, to specific denominations, and to religious doctrine. Evangelicals believe in the importance of personal salvation through Jesus Christ, usually through a born-again experience, in the inerrancy of the Bible, and in the importance of spreading the gospel.

Family Research Council Organization of the contemporary Christian Right, headed by Gary Bauer. The FRC was once the political arm of Focus on the Family, although the two groups are now separate for tax reasons. The FRC specializes in providing detailed research on policy issues.

Flying Fundamentalists Arm of the Defenders of the Christian Faith that dispatched squadrons of speakers to antievolution rallies in the Midwest. In 1926 the Flying Fundamentalists appeared in more than 200 cities in Minnesota alone.

Focus on the Family Radio ministry and organization of the contemporary Christian Right, headed by James Dobson.

Free exercise clause Phrase in First Amendment that is source of controversy regarding religious liberty: "Congress shall make no law . . . prohibiting the free exercise thereof [religion]."

Fundamentalist Term used to describe a religious movement, specific denominations and churches, and religious doctrine. Fundamentalists believe in the importance of remaining separate from the world, in the literal truth of the Bible, and in the importance of personal salvation.

Glossolalia Commonly known as "speaking in tongues." Religious practice in which individual speaks in no known human language. Some individuals believe they speak in the language of angels; others think they are worshiping in their own private language with God.

Home School Legal Defense Association Organization that defends rights of homeschooling parents, most of whom are Christian conservatives. The HSLDA is headed by Michael Farris.

Libertarian (First Amendment)   Individual who believes that free exercise of religion should not be limited. Libertarians generally hold that religious liberty should supersede secular law and that laws that have the effect of limiting the religious practice of one or more groups should have religious exemptions.

Menorah   Jewish candelabrum displayed during Hanukkah.

Moral Majority   Premier Christian Right group of the 1980s, headed by Jerry Falwell. The Moral Majority established paper organizations in all states but was primarily a direct-mail organization that received substantial media attention.

National Association of Evangelicals   Organization of evangelical denominations, formed by neoevangelicals in 1942 and active today.

Neoevangelicalism   Term used to describe religious movement and religious doctrine. Neoevangelicals rejected the militant separatism of the fundamentalists and encouraged an engagement with the modern world.

Old Time Gospel Hour   Jerry Falwell's televised sermons from the Liberty Baptist Church in Lynchburg, Virginia.

Operation Rescue   Antiabortion group that specializes in blockading abortion clinics. Members try to prevent women from entering the clinics by physically blocking their path and by harassing them verbally. The organization attracts members of Christian Right groups but also a few pro-life liberals.

Oregon Citizens Alliance   Organization of the contemporary Christian Right that continues to attempt to amend the Oregon constitution to allow job discrimination against gays and lesbians and to condemn homosexuality.

Party faction   Identifiable group within a political party that fields its own candidates for intraparty nomination contests and usually has an identifiable ideology as well.

Pentecostal   Term used to describe religious movement, specific denominations, and religious doctrine. Pentecostals believe in the second blessing of the Holy Spirit and in worship that includes ecstatic practices such as speaking in tongues. Unlike charismatics, pentecostals are found in specific denominations.

People for the American Way   Organization founded by Norman Lear to oppose the Christian Right.

Postmillennialism   The doctrinal belief that the millennial kingdom will occur before Christ comes again. The implication of the doctrine is that political action may improve the world and hasten the millennium.

Premillennialism   The doctrinal belief that the millennial kingdom will occur after Christ comes again. Premillennialists believe that the condition of the world must worsen until Christ comes again. The implication of the doctrine is that political action is somewhat futile.

Pro-family   Term preferred by some Christian Right groups to describe their movement.

Religious nonpreferentialist   Individual who takes an accommodationist position on the establishment clause of the First Amendment and a libertarian position on the free exercise clause. A religious nonpreferentialist seeks a more open display of Christian and other religious symbols and practices.

Religious Roundtable   Christian Right group from the 1980s.

Scopes trial   Also known as the "Great Monkey Trial," the trial of John Scopes for teaching evolution in Dayton, Tennessee, embarrassed fundamentalists and led them to retreat from politics, but it also led textbook publishers to retreat from including evolution in biology texts.

Secular humanism   Philosophy that centers on human values and denies the influence of supernatural forces such as gods. Although the American Humanist Association has a membership of around 5,000, Christian Right activists depict secular humanism as a militant religious system that wants to destroy Christianity. In fundamentalist circles, secular humanism is a very broad, vague concept.

Separationist   Person who believes that the First Amendment establishment clause mandates that government not become entangled in religion in any way and remain neutral between religion and secularism.

Separatism   Doctrinal belief of fundamentalists that Christians should remain apart from the world.

700 Club   Pat Robertson's television program, which features interviews with guests of varied religious backgrounds, an African-American cohost, and political commentary by Robertson. The *700 Club* provided the financial nucleus of Robertson's 1988 presidential campaign.

Social conservatives   Americans who take conservative positions on issues such as abortion, gay rights, and school prayer.

Social gospel   Doctrine in the early twentieth century that the church should focus its efforts on helping alleviate social problems.

Stealth candidates   Candidates who hide their ties to the Christian Right until after the election. Although stealth candidacies were once encouraged, most Christian Right groups now advise their activists to acknowledge their connections with the movement if asked but to concentrate their campaigns on other issues.

Traditional Values Coalition   Organization of the contemporary Christian Right, headed by Louis Sheldon. TVC focuses primarily on opposing laws that protect gays and lesbians from job discrimination.

Voter guides   Materials distributed by Christian Right and other groups providing information on the policy positions of candidates. If voter guides are produced by tax-exempt groups, they must be nonpartisan.

World's Christian Fundamentals Association   Religious group formed in 1919 to provide structure to the fundamentalist religious movement. The WCFA provided resources for the formation of the antievolution groups of the 1920s.

Notes

Chapter 1

1. Whether "family values night" at the GOP convention hurt the Republicans is the subject of some debate. See Cromartie, 1994; Abramowitz, 1995.

2. Personal communication via e-mail, September 1994.

3. Although most movement leaders explicitly include Jews in their discussion of the American religious tradition, others do not. Mississippi Governor Kirk Fordice attracted praise and rebuke when he refused to change his statement that the United States was a Christian nation to a claim that it was a Judeo-Christian nation. The statement was made to GOP governors in November 1992.

4. See the case studies in Rozell and Wilcox, 1995a, 1997, and in Green, Rozell, and Wilcox, 2000; see also Wilcox, Green, and Rozell, 1995.

5. For an overview of public attitudes on these issues, see Jelen and Wilcox, 1995.

6. Robertson, 1992.

7. All movement leaders now eschew stealth tactics, although many opponents remain convinced that school board candidates frequently attempt to disguise their ties to the movement.

8. "Equal Rights Initiative in Iowa Attacked," *Washington Post*, August 23, 1995, p. A15.

9. Cited in ibid., p. 20.

10. *Christian Coalition Leadership Manual*, p. 13. Cited in "A Campaign of Falsehoods," a special report of the Christian Coalition, July 28, 1994.

11. "A Campaign of Falsehoods," p. 17.

12. See especially the publication "The Freedom Writer," published by the Institute for First Amendment Studies, Great Barrington, MA.

13. Quoted in *Atlanta Journal and Constitution*, December 14, 1994.

14. A prominent exception is A. James Reichley (1985), who argued that theistic-humanist religions provide the proper values to mold a good society.

15. The Williamsburg Charter survey, conducted in 1988, indicated that more than 85 percent would vote for candidates from all religious traditions but only a third would support an atheist, even if the person were from their party and shared their political views.

16. Data are from National Election Study, 1992; Miller et al., 1992.

17. In the 1992 and 1993 General Social Surveys (GSS), nearly one in six Catholics who attend church weekly took a strict pro-choice position, supporting abortion in each of six concrete circumstances. More than 40 percent took a strict pro-life position, with the plurality favoring legal abortions in some but not all circumstances. Davis and Smith, 1994.

Chapter 2

1. These doctrinal differences have important implications for the policy positions of evangelicals. Guth et al., 1995, have shown that premillennialists are less likely to support environmental protection. If Christ will soon come again, why worry about a little pollution? On the other hand, postmillennialists may support environmental legislation, arguing that God created the snail darter and it therefore should be present during the millennium that ushers in the kingdom of heaven.

2. See Acts 2:1–23.

3. There is some dispute among pentecostals as to just how many blessings exist. For many, speaking in tongues is part of a third blessing, but for the Assemblies of God it is part of a second blessing.

4. Speaking in tongues generally involves one or more members of a congregation speaking in what the nonbeliever would deem nonsense syllables. Two somewhat different explanations are usually offered by those within the tradition: They are speaking the "language of the angels," or they are speaking different private languages that exist between God and his believers. Being "slain in the Spirit" generally involves falling to the floor, often after the loss of consciousness. In charismatic and pentecostal services, strong men identify those who are likely to be slain and move to catch them as they fall.

5. The biblical account of the Pentecost in the second chapter of Acts describes the apostles speaking in tongues, so that members of the polynational audience all heard the sermon in their native language. For fundamentalists, this gift was given in the early days of the church to further its evangelical mission. The "tongues" were real, earthly languages.

6. For a detailed discussion, see Furniss, 1963.

7. For a detailed account of the bills, see Furniss, 1963. See also Hunter, 1987.

8. Some continued to exist, however. The Christian Anti-Communism Crusade was still mailing literature as late as 1990.

9. The church now has 22,000 members. For more information, see http://www.trbc.org/.

10. Quoted in Harrell, 1988, p. 140.

11. The Michigan process was a complex, multistage affair, and there was no real counting of delegates after the first stage. But journalists and political professionals polled delegates for the second stage who claimed Robertson was comfortably ahead of Bush. Eventually, however, the Bush forces joined with those who backed Jack Kemp and managed to seize control.

12. For an interesting account of the Robertson campaign, see Hertzke, 1993.

13. For a well-argued example, see Bruce, 1988.

14. Anticommunism played its least important role in the Robertson campaign, although Robertson's claim of secret missiles in Cuba hearkened to the earlier, more conspiratorial accounts of communism.

15. Quoted in Rozell and Wilcox, 1996.

16. For the biblical referents to the term "born again," see John 3:5–8; I Peter 1:23. For many evangelicals, the born-again experience is a sudden one, marked by an emotional re-

lease. Evangelicals in this tradition can usually recite the date and circumstances when they were reborn. For others, it is a gradual process.

17. The "other evangelicals" category is quite heterogeneous. It includes moderate neo-evangelicals, Anabaptists from peace churches, and members of Holiness churches.

18. This is especially a problem in the South, where most citizens claim to be born again.

19. For example, surveys show a relatively high portion of churchgoers call themselves fundamentalists, and many of these do not support any fundamentalist doctrine.

20. For example, nearly 9 percent of Catholics are charismatics, according to this same survey.

21. David Leege, in personal communication, noted that most surveys do not include items suited to measuring religiosity among Catholics. Catholics read their Bible less often than evangelicals in part because Bible reading is not a major part of Catholic religiosity.

Chapter 3

1. There is some disagreement among scholars as to whether the Eagle Forum is a Christian Right organization. Schlafly is Catholic, as are many women in the organization, and the group did base much of its opposition to the ERA on antistatist appeals that the government should not interfere in the relationship between men and women. But much of the organization's literature links its antifeminism to biblical and other religious arguments.

2. Groups that have taken such positions include the now-defunct Just Life political action committee (Bendyna, 1993) and Common Concern (Maxwell, 1994).

3. The Washington Post reported in April that the college is drawing far fewer applicants than expected.

4. There is obviously no biblical warrant for opposition to gun control, but in the South many Christian conservatives speak of the "God-given right to carry a gun." Bates (1993) reported that Christian conservative parents who objected to what they perceived to be antibiblical passages in a school text listed among the objectionable passages one that endorsed gun control.

5. For a detailed account, see Lunch, 1995.

6. Virginia's sodomy laws prohibit homosexual relations and some kinds of sexual relations among heterosexuals as well.

7. Robert O'Harrow Jr., "Christian Group's Push Felt in Move Against Gay Paper," *Washington Post*, October 1, 1993, p. D2.

8. Burl Gilyard, "Fake Wobegon," *New Republic*, September 12, 1994, p. 20.

9. Approximately a third of the members of the state central committee are Christian Right supporters, a third are moderates who oppose the Christian Right, and a third are neutral toward the movement. A majority of the neutral members are strong conservatives who work with Christian conservatives, which gives the Christian Right a working majority on the committee (Rozell and Wilcox, 1996).

10. Jim Toler, 1994. "Local GOP Shifts Toward the Right," *Fredericksburg Free Lance Star*, March 29, 1994, pp. 1, 3.

11. Cited in Hertzke, 1993, p. 149.

12. Surveys show that although most Americans want their president to have strong religious beliefs, many are quite leery of voting for a minister. See Jelen and Wilcox, 1995.

13. Ultimately, however, Robertson lost because voters did not like him or his message.

14. This is not always true: In 1986, when a moderate Republican, Ed Zchau, ran against the incumbent, Alan Cranston, for one of California's U.S. Senate seats, an independent Christian Right candidate pulled enough votes to deny Zchau the victory.

15. For example, the guides listed Robb as in favor of taxpayer funding of obscene art and North as opposed. Yet Robb had voted for the controversial Helms amendment to cut the National Endowment for the Arts budget and restrict federal funding of offensive art. The guides said that Robb opposed voluntary school prayer when he clearly was on record favoring the idea.

16. For an account of the earlier PACs, see Wilcox, 1988a.

17. Lottery referenda generate interesting coalitions. Christian Right activists oppose lotteries on moral grounds, whereas liberal churches and citizens oppose them because they are a revenue source that draws disproportionately from the poor.

18. Wald, 1992. Of course, the parable of the good steward would seem to suggest that when Christ returns, someone will be accountable for the failure of the snail darter or the spotted owl to prosper.

19. Moen, 1990. But Moen correctly noted that Christian Right issues were not highlighted in Reagan's State of the Union addresses and that his endorsement of the agenda was not especially ringing.

20. Farris, 1992, p. 43.

21. For core evangelicals the correlation between feelings toward the Court and feelings toward liberals was .35 and with feelings toward conservatives was negative .05. For non-evangelicals and African Americans, the correlations were .2 for both liberals and conservatives.

22. Religious groups have also become far more active in filing amicus briefs. For an overview of legal activity by religious groups, see Ivers, 1990; 1992.

23. See Spencer S. Hsu, "Revised Social Studies Standards for Virginia Schools Dropped; Teacher Opposition Cited," *Washington Post*, April 27, 1995, p. A8.

Chapter 4

1. The John Birch Society was secular only in comparison with the explicitly fundamentalist Right. It had strong constituencies among fundamentalists and conservative Catholics. See Grupp, 1969.

2. See, for example, the essays in Schoenberger, 1969.

3. Pat Robertson's writings echo some of these more eccentric theories.

4. Adorno et al., 1950.

5. Wilcox, Jelen, and Linzey, 1991.

6. Wilcox, 1992; Rozell and Wilcox, 1996. But leaders of the Christian Right of the 1980s made a number of statements that outraged Jewish groups, including the re-

mark at a Religious Roundtable meeting in August by the Reverend Bailey Smith, then the president of the Southern Baptist Convention, that "God does not hear the prayer of a Jew."

7. Jelen, 1991a.

8. Conover and Gray, 1981, p. 4.

9. For a description of how churches can dominate social networks, see Ammerman, 1987.

10. Wilcox, 1992.

11. In fact, some researchers have argued that membership in any group that seeks to alter public policy to benefit all citizens is in one sense irrational. From an economic perspective, it is far more logical for individuals to be "free riders," in the hope that the group succeeds without investing their own time and money. It is highly unlikely that ten hours a week or $25 a year will make any difference in the success of the group, and citizens will benefit from the policies enacted whether or not they have contributed to the group's efforts. Yet many citizens are active in political organizations and give their time and money even when they believe that theirs is a lost cause. Many enjoy interacting with others who share their views, and others feel motivated to help pursue their policy goals because of a sense of obligation or because they derive great pleasure from their occasional political victories.

12. See, for example, *The Two Faces of the Christian Coalition,* a pamphlet published by People for the American Way.

13. See, for example, Verba and Nie, 1972.

14. When white evangelicals are compared with others of similar education, income, and age levels, the turnout gap is quite small and is not statistically significant.

15. Exodus 22:18.

16. Thanks to John Green for providing these data.

17. Political scientist John Green, who provided these data, has argued instead that Christian Right elites would be less likely to protect civil liberties but not more likely to limit them.

18. Family Research Council, March 9, 1994, p. 2.

19. Warren, 1993; 1996.

20. The Catholic church does not permit abortions to save the life of the mother, but most Protestants in the movement would allow this exception while setting strict limits on doctors to certify that there is a real and present danger.

21. In fact, it is unlikely that the passage in question is even about abortion. Verse 12 states that "He that smiteth a man, so that he die, shall be surely put to death." This verse clearly prescribes the death penalty for murder. But the verses that Christian Right activists claim speak of abortion are much more ambiguous. Verses 22 and 23 state that "If men strive, and hurt a woman with child, so that her fruit depart from her, and yet no mischief follow, he shall be surely punished, according as the woman's husband shall lay upon him: and he shall pay as the judges determine. And if any mischief follow, then thou shalt give life for life." Thus if the woman lives, the penalty appears to be a fine as determined by the husband. Yet if this were a voluntary abortion with a husband's consent, that fine would

surely be minuscule or nonexistent. Moreover, the death penalty is not invoked if the "fruit" departs, although this same chapter mandates the death penalty for poorly fencing in an aggressive ox that later escapes and kills someone.

22. Transcript of ABC *Nightline* program, "God and the Grassroots," November 4, 1993.

23. "People and Events," *Church and State*, April 1988, p. 14.

24. For an account of a Christian school associated with a fundamentalist church, see Ammerman, 1987.

25. The survey data also do not reveal whether some would prefer that creationism be taught in literature or religion classes.

26. Pat Robertson noted on the *700 Club* on February 26, 1987, "As a seventeen-, sixteen-year-old, the maximum sex urges running through a young boy, and you give him pictures . . . positive homosexual and lesbian relationships with pictures and the whole thing. . . . that's going to get his juices coursing through him, and he's going to be looking for sex partners as fast as he can."

27. For a detailed discussion, see Morken, 1994.

28. Interestingly, this was the position of the first wave of gay rights activists, although many now believe that sexual orientation is fixed by genes or socialization.

29. Interestingly, many Christian Right activists favor repealing the earned income tax credit for poor families, which would lower the incomes of poor families and by the same logic force more women into the labor force.

30. This does not mean, of course, that Christian conservatives advocate spousal abuse. Indeed, Christian conservatives counsel men to offer great respect and support for their wives and advise wives to obey their husbands. Some Christian Right leaders object to spousal abuse laws because they believe they could be misused or provide a wedge for greater government interference into the privacy of families.

31. Sources for these data are the General Social Survey (GSS) and the American National Election Studies (NES).

32. In both cases, the survey questions were worded in such a way as to make the conservative response more difficult. The questions asked respondents to agree or disagree with "The government should not regulate what adults read, even if it includes pornography."

33. Cited in Shupe, 1989, p. 25.

34. Cited in Neuhaus, 1991.

35. Matthew 19:23–24; see also Mark 10:24–26; Luke 18:25. The eye of the needle was an entry to the walled cities of Israel, which camels could enter only with great difficulty, crawling on their knees. Interestingly, the Bible does not contain any passage that says "blessed are the rich, for only they shall receive health care."

Chapter 5

1. Cited in Lienesch, 1994, p. 243. Presumably Robertson's birthday party that year will require some very careful planning and may draw a very large crowd.

2. Respondents were asked if they were members of various kinds of political groups. Members of the Christian Right are those who indicated they were members of Christian conservative groups.

3. Many activists quote with approval II Timothy 4:7, "I have fought a good fight, I have finished my course, I have kept the faith."

4. There are some Christian reconstructionists who are willing to dominate society by force, but they constitute the fringe of the movement.

5. Personal communication via e-mail, October 2, 1995.

6. Personal communication via e-mail, October 10, 1995.

7. Personal communication via e-mail, September 14, 1995.

8. Cited in Cromartie, 1994, p. 36.

References

Abramowitz, Alan. 1995. "It's Abortion, Stupid: Policy Voting in the 1992 Presidential Election." *Journal of Politics* 57:176–186.

Adorno, T. W., Else Frenkel-Brunswik, Daniel J. Levinson, and R. Nevitt Sanford. 1950. *The Authoritarian Personality*. New York: Harper and Row.

Ammerman, Nancy Tatom. 1987. *Bible Believers: Fundamentalists in the Modern World*. New Brunswick, NJ: Rutgers University Press.

Andolina, Molly W., and Clyde Wilcox. 2000. "The Paradoxes of Popularity: Public Support for Bill Clinton During the Lewinsky Scandal" (with Molly Sonner). In Mark J. Rozell and Clyde Wilcox (eds.), *The Clinton Scandal and the future of American Government*. Washington, DC: Georgetown University Press.

Barber, Benjamin R. 1984. *Strong Democracy: Participatory Politics for a New Age*. Berkeley: University of California Press.

Barkun, Michael. 1994. *Religion and the Racist Right*. Chapel Hill: University of North Carolina Press.

Barrett, Greg. 1999. "Why James Dobson's $120 Million Ministry Is a Household Name." *The Detroit News*, May 3, A12.

Bates, Stephen. 1993. *Battleground*. New York: Henry Holt.

———. 1995. "The Christian Coalition Nobody Knows." *Weekly Standard*, September 25.

Bendyna, Mary. 1994. "JustLife Action." In R. Biersack, P. Herrnson, and C. Wilcox (eds.), *Risky Business: PAC Decisionmaking in Congressional Elections*. Armonk, NY: M. E. Sharpe.

———. 1995. "Catholics and the Christian Coalition." Presented at the annual meeting of the Association for the Sociology of Religion, Washington, DC.

Bendyna, Mary, John C. Green, Mark J. Rozell, and Clyde Wilcox. 2000. "Catholics and the Christian Right: A View from Four States." *Journal for the Scientific Study of Religion*. Forthcoming.

Berry, Jeffrey M., Kent E. Portney, and Ken Thomson. 1993. *The Rebirth of Urban Democracy*. Washington, DC: Brookings.

Blakeman, Bruce W. nd. "Report of Survey of Concerned Women of America Members and of Randomly Selected Women." Concerned Women of America, issued in 1996.

Blumenthal, Sidney. 1994. "Christian Soldiers." *New Yorker* 70, July 18:31–37.

Brin, David. 1994. *Otherness*. New York: Bantam Books.

Broder, David S. 1995. "Christian Group Flexes Newfound Muscles." *Washington Post*, September 10:A1, A24.

Brown, Clifford W., Jr., Lynda W. Powell, and Clyde Wilcox. 1994. *Presidential Contributor Study*. Computer data file.

———. 1995. *Serious Money: Fundraising and Contributing in Presidential Nomination Campaigns*. New York: Cambridge University Press.

Bruce, Steve. 1988. *The Rise and Fall of the New Christian Right: Conservative Protestant Politics in America 1978–1988*. Oxford: Oxford University Press.

Bruce, Steve, Peter Kivisto, and William Swatos Jr. 1994. *The Rapture of Politics: The Christian Right as the United States Approaches the Year 2000*. New Brunswick, NJ: Transaction Press.

Cole, Stewart. 1931. *The History of Fundamentalism*. Westport, CT: Greenwood Press.

Conover, Pamela, and Virginia Gray. 1981. "Political Activists and Conflict over Abortion and ERA: Pro-Family vs. Pro-Woman." Presented at the annual meeting of the Midwest Political Science Association, Chicago.

Cook, Elizabeth Adell, Ted G. Jelen, and Clyde Wilcox. 1992. *Between Two Absolutes: Public Opinion and the Politics of Abortion*. Boulder, CO: Westview.

———. 1993. "Generational Differences in Attitudes Toward Abortion." In M. Goggin (ed.), *Understanding the New Politics of Abortion*. Beverly Hills, CA: Sage.

———. 1994. "Issue Voting in Gubernatorial Elections: Abortion and Post-Webster Politics." *Journal of Politics* 56:187–199.

Cromartie, Michael (ed.). 1994. *Disciples and Democracy: Religious Conservatives and the Future of American Politics*. Washington, DC: Ethics and Public Policy Center.

Davis, James Allan, and Tom W. Smith. 1994. *General Social Surveys, 1972–1994*. Computer data file.

Deckman, Melissa M. 1999. *Christian Soldiers on Local Battlefields: Campaigning for Control of America's School Boards*. Unpublished Ph.D. Dissertation, The American University.

Dillon, S. 1993a. "Catholics Join Bid by Conservatives for School Boards." *New York Times*, April 16.

———. 1993b. "Fundamentalists and Catholics." *New York Times*, November 14:6.

Dodson, Debra L. 1990. "Socialization of Party Activists: National Convention Delegates, 1972–1981." *American Journal of Political Science* 34:1119–1141.

Edsall, Thomas B. 1995. "Robertson Urges Christian Activists to Take Over GOP." *Washington Post*, September 10:A24.

Falwell, Jerry. 1981. *The Fundamentalist Phenomenon*. Garden City, NJ: Doubleday.

Farris, Michael P. 1992. *Where Do I Draw the Line?* Minneapolis: Bethany House.

Finke, Roger, and Rodney Stark. 1992. *The Churching of America, 1776–1992*. New Brunswick, NJ: Rutgers University Press.

Furniss, Norman. 1963. *The Fundamentalist Controversy, 1918–1931*. Hamden, CT: Archdon Books.

Gamble, Barbara S. 1995. "Putting Civil Rights to a Popular Vote." Unpublished mauscript.

Georgianna, Sharon Linzey. 1988. *Moral Majority Survey*. Computer data file.

———. 1989. *The Moral Majority and Fundamentalism: Plausibility and Dissonance*. Lewiston, NY: Edwin Mellon Press.

Gimpel, James G. 1994. *Risky Business? PAC Decisionmaking in Congressional Elections*. Armonk, NY: M. E. Sharpe.

Goodstein, Laurie. 1999. "Coalitions's Woes May Hinder Goals Of Christian Right." *New York Times on the Web*, August 2.

Green, John C. 1995. "The Christian Right and the 1994 Elections: An Overview." In M. Rozell and C. Wilcox (eds.), *God at the Grassroots: The Christian Right in the 1994 Elections*. Lanham, MD: Rowman & Littlefield.

———. 2000. "The Christian Right and the 1998 Elections: An Overview." In John C. Green, Mark J. Rozell, and Clyde Wilcox (eds.), *Prayers in the Precincts*. Washington, DC: Georgetown U Press.

Green, John C., and James L. Guth. 1988. "The Christian Right in the Republican Party: The Case of Pat Robertson's Contributors." *Journal of Politics* 50:150–165.

Green, John C., James L. Guth, Lyman A. Kellstedt, and Corwin E. Smidt. 1990–1991. *Survey of Religious Activists, 1990–1991*. Computer data file.

———. 1992. *National Survey of Religion and Politics, 1992*. Computer data file.

———. 1994. "Uncivil Challengers? Support for Civil Liberties Among Religious Activists." *Journal of Political Science* 24:25–49.

Green, John C., James L. Guth, and Clyde Wilcox. 1995. "The Christian Right in State Republican Parties." Presented at the annual meeting of the Midwest Political Science Association, Chicago.

———. 1998. "The Social Movement Meets the Party: The Christian Right in the GOP." In Anne Costain and Andrew S. McFarland (eds.), *Social Movements and American Political Institutions*. Lanham, MD: Rowman & Littlefield.

Green, John C., Lyman Kellstedt, Corwin Smidt, and James L. Guth. 1992. "National Survey of American Evangelicals." Ray C. Bliss Institute of Applied Politics and Survey Research, University of Akron.

Grupp, Fred. 1969. "The Political Perspectives of the John Birch Society Members." In R. Schoenberger (ed.), *The American Right Wing*. New York: Holt, Rinehart, and Winston.

Guth, James L. 1983. "The Politics of the Christian Right." In A. Cigler and B. Loomis (eds.), *Interest Group Politics*. Washington, DC: CQ Press.

Guth, James L., John C. Green, Lyman A. Kellstedt, and Corwin E. Smidt. 1995. "Faith and the Environment: Religious Beliefs and Attitudes on Environmental Policy." *American Journal of Political Science* 39:364–382.

Guth, James L., and Lyman A. Kellstedt. 1999. "Religion on Capitol Hill: The Case of the House of Representatives in the 105th Congress." Presented at the Biennial Meeting of Christians in Political Science, Calvin College, Grand Rapids, MI.

Hadden, Jeffery K., Anson Shupe, James Hawdon, and Kenneth Martin. 1987. "Why Jerry Falwell Killed the Moral Majority." In M. Fishwick and R. Browne (eds.), *The God Pumpers: Religion in the Electronic Age*. Bowling Green, OH: Popular Press.

Haider-Markel, Donald P., and Kenneth J. Meier. 1996. "The Politics of Gay and Lesbian Rights: Expanding the Scope of the Conflict." *Journal of Politics*.150:47–62.

Hale, John. 1995. "Mainers Face Off on Gays." *Bangor Daily News*, October 28:14.

Harrell, David E. 1988. *Pat Robertson: A Personal, Religious, and Political Portrait.* San Francisco: Harper and Row.

Hertzke, Allen. 1988. *Representing God in Washington: The Role of Religious Lobbies in the American Polity.* Knoxville: University of Tennessee Press.

———. 1993. *Echoes of Discontent: Jesse Jackson, Pat Robertson, and the Resurgence of Populism.* Washington, DC: CQ Press.

Hunter, James Davison. 1987. "The Evangelical Worldview Since 1890." In R. Neuhaus and M. Cromartie (eds.), *Piety and Politics.* Washington, DC: Ethics and Public Policy Center.

———. 1991. *Culture Wars: The Struggle to Define America.* New York: Basic Books.

Ivers, Gregg. 1990. "Organized Religion and the Supreme Court." *Journal of Church and State* 32:775–793.

———. 1992. "Religious Organizations as Constitutional Litigants." *Polity* 25:243–266.

Jacobs, Mike. 1995. "A Tale of Two Cities: Christian Right Activism in the New York City and Vista, California, School Districts." Unpublished manuscript.

Jacoby, Mary. 1999. "What Has She Done to the Christian Coalition?" *St. Petersburg Times,* October 3, a1.

Jelen, Ted G. 1990. *The Political Mobilization of Religious Belief.* New York: Greenwood.

———. 1991a. "Religion and Democratic Citizenship: A Review Essay." *Polity* 23:471–481.

———. 1991b. *The Political Mobilization of Religious Beliefs.* New York: Praeger.

Jelen, Ted G., and Clyde Wilcox. 1995. *Public Attitudes Toward Church and State.* Armonk, NY: M. E. Sharpe.

Jorstad, Erling. 1970. *The Politics of Doomsday.* Nashville, TN: Abingdon Press.

Kellstedt, Lyman. 1989. "The Meaning and Measurement of Evangelicalism: Problems and Prospects." In T. Jelen (ed.), *Religion and Political Behavior in the United States.* New York: Praeger.

Koeppen, Sheilah. 1969. "The Radical Right and the Politics of Consensus." In R. Schoenberger (ed.), *The American Right Wing.* New York: Holt, Rinehart, and Winston.

Levy, Leonard W. 1986. *The Establishment Clause.* New York: Macmillan.

Lewis, Gregory B., and Jonathan L. Edelson. 2000. "DOMA and ENDA: Congress Votes on Gay Rights." In Craig A. Rimmerman, Kenneth D. Wald, and Clyde Wilcox (eds.), *The Politics of Gay Rights.* Chicago: University of Chicago Press.

Liebman, Robert C. 1983. "Mobilizing the Moral Majority." In R. Liebman and R. Wuthnow (eds.), *The New Christian Right: Mobilization and Legitimation.* New York: Aldine.

———. 1995. "New Perspectives on the New Christian Right." Presented at the annual meeting of the American Sociological Association, Washington, DC.

Lienesch, Michael. 1994. *Redeeming America.* Chapel Hill: University of North Carolina Press.

———. 1995. "Mobilizing Against Modernity: The World's Christian Fundamentals Association and the Fundamentalist Movement." Presented at the annual meeting of the American Political Science Association, Chicago.

Lunch, William. 1995. "Oregon: Identity and Politics in the Northwest." In M. Rozell and C. Wilcox (eds.), *God at the Grassroots.* Lanham, MD: Rowman & Littlefield.

Malbin, Michael. 1978. *Religion and Politics: The Intentions of the Authors of the First Amendment.* Washington, DC: AEI Press.

Marsden, George. 1980. *Fundamentalism and American Culture.* New York: Oxford University Press.

Maxwell, Carol J. C. 1994. "Meaning and Motivation in Pro-Life Direct Action." Unpublished Ph.D. dissertation, Washington University, St. Louis, MO.

Mill, John Stuart. 1862. *Considerations on Representative Government.* New York: Harper and Brothers.

Miller, Warren E., Donald Kinder, Stephen Rosenstone, and the National Election Studies. 1992. *American National Election Study, 1992.* Computer file.

Millsaps, Rhett. 1999. "Loving the Sinner and Hating the Sin: The Emerging Ex-Gay Movement in Christian Right Politics." Unpublished manuscript.

Moen, Matthew. 1989. *The Christian Right and Congress.* Tuscaloosa: University of Alabama Press.

———. 1990. "Ronald Reagan and the Social Issues: Rhetorical Support for the Christian Right." *Social Science Journal* 27:199–207.

———. 1992. *The Transformation of the Christian Right.* Tuscaloosa: University of Alabama Press.

———. 1994. "From Revolution to Evolution: The Changing Nature of the Christian Right." In S. Bruce, P. Kivisto, and W. Swatos (eds.), *The Rapture of Politics.* New Brunswick, NJ: Transaction Press.

———. 1995. "The Christian Right in the Twenty-first Century." Presented at the annual meeting of the Northeastern Political Science Association, Newark, NJ.

Morken, Hubert. 1994. "'No Special Rights': The Thinking Strategy Behind Colorado's Amendment #2 Strategy." Presented at the annual meeting of the American Political Science Association, New York.

Neuhaus, Richard. 1991. "The Theonomist Temptation." *First Things* 35:151–155.

Numbers, Ronald N. 1992. *The Creationists.* New York: Alfred A. Knopf.

Nunn, C., H. Crockett, and J. A. Williams. 1978. *Tolerance for Nonconformity.* San Francisco: Jossey-Bass.

O'Hara, Thomas J. 1989. "The Civil Rights Restoration Act: The Role of Religious Lobbies." Presented at the annual meeting of the American Political Science Association, Atlanta.

People for the American Way. 1995. *The Two Faces of the Christian Coalition.*

Persinos, John F. 1994. "Has the Christian Right Taken Over the Republican Party?" *Campaigns and Elections,* September:21–24.

Quebedeaux, Richard. 1983. *The New Charismatics II.* New York: Harper and Row.

Randolph, E. 1993. "In NY School Board 'Holy War,' Vote Is Split but Civics Triumph." *Washington Post,* May 22:A5.

Reed, Douglas S. 1998. "I Can Play That: Social Movement Repertoires and State Constitutional Politics." Presented at the annual meeting of the American Political Science Association, Boston.

Reed, Ralph. 1994a. *Politically Incorrect: The Emerging Faith Factor in American Politics.* Dallas: Word Publishing.

————. 1994b. "What Do Religious Conservatives Really Want?" In Michael Cromartie (ed.), *Disciples and Democracy*. Washington, DC: Ethics and Public Policy Center.

Reichley, A. James. 1985. *Religion in American Public Life*. Washington, DC: Brookings.

Ribuffo, Leo. 1983. *The Old Christian Right*. Philadelphia: Temple University Press.

Robertson, Pat. 1992. *The New World Order*. Dallas: Word Publishing.

Rozell, Mark J., and Clyde Wilcox (eds.). 1995a. *God at the Grassroots: The Christian Right in the 1994 Elections*. Lanham, MD: Rowman & Littlefield.

Rozell, Mark, and Clyde Wilcox. 1995b. *Virginia Delegate Survey*. Computer data file.

————. 1996. *Second Coming: The New Christian Right in Virginia Politics*. Baltimore: The Johns Hopkins University Press.

————. 1997. *God at the Grassroots, 1996: The Christian Right in the 1996 Elections*. Lanham, MD: Rowman & Littlefield.

————. 2000. "Virginia: Prophet in Waiting?" In John C. Green, Mark J. Rozell, and Clyde Wilcox (eds.), *Prayers in the Precincts*. Washington, DC: Georgetown U Press.

Sandeen, Ernest. 1970. *The Roots of Fundamentalism*. Chicago: University of Chicago Press.

Schoenberger, Robert. 1969. *The American Right Wing*. New York: Holt, Rinehart, and Winston.

Shupe, Anson. 1989. "The Reconstructionist Movement in the New Christian Right." *Christian Century* 106:880–882.

Sigelman, Lee, Clyde Wilcox, and Emmett Buell. 1987. "An Unchanged Minority: Popular Support for the Moral Majority in 1980 and 1984." *Social Science Quarterly* 68:876–884.

Smidt, Corwin. 1980. "Civil Religious Orientations Among Elementary School Children." *Sociological Analysis* 41:25–40.

Sniderman, Paul M., Richard A. Brody, and Philip E. Tetlock. 1991. *Reasoning and Choice: Explorations in Political Psychology*. New York: Cambridge University Press.

Stouffer, Samuel A. 1955. *Communism, Conformity, and Civil Liberties*. New York: Doubleday.

Suczek, Yohanna M. 1995. "Christ, the Internet, and You." Unpublished manuscript.

Sullivan, Robert. 1993. "An Army of the Faithful." *New York Times Magazine,* April 25:32–35, 40–44.

Thomas, Cal, and Ed Dobson. 1999. *Blinded by Might: Can the Religious Right Save America?* Grand Rapids: Zondervan.

Tocqueville, Alexis de. 1945. *Democracy in America*. P. Bradley (ed.). 2 vols. New York: Vintage Books.

Verba, Sidney, and Norman Nie. 1972. *Participation in America: Political Democracy and Social Equality*. Cambridge: Harvard University Press.

Wald, Kenneth J. 1992. *Religion and Politics in the United States*. 2d ed. Washington, DC: CQ Press.

Wald, Kenneth J., Dennis Owen, and Samuel Hill. 1988. "Churches as Political Communities." *American Political Science Review* 82:531–549.

Warren, Mark. 1993. "New Patterns of Politicization: Implications for Participatory Democratic Theory." Presented at the annual meeting of the American Political Science Association, Washington, DC.

———. 1996. "Deliberative Democracy and Authority." *American Political Science Review.* 139:96–115.

Wesskopf, Michael. 1993. "'Gospel Grapevine' Displays Strength in Controversy over Gay Ban." *Washington Post,* February 1:A10.

Whitley, Tyler. 1994. "GOP Factions Square Off at Local Level." *Richmond Times-Dispatch,* April 30:A1, 8.

Wilcox, Clyde. 1987. "Popular Support for the Moral Majority in 1980: A Second Look." *Social Science Quarterly* 68:157–167.

———. 1988a. "Political Action Committees of the New Christian Right: A Longitudinal Analysis." *Journal for the Scientific Study of Religion* 27:60–71.

———. 1988b. "American Religion and Politics in Comparative Perspective." Presented at the annual meeting of the World Congress on Sociology, Madrid.

———. 1992. *God's Warriors: The Christian Right in 20th Century America.* Baltimore: The Johns Hopkins University Press.

———. 1995. *The Latest American Revolution?* New York: St. Martin's.

Wilcox, Clyde, Matthew DeBell, and Lee Sigelman, 1999. "The Second Coming of the New Christian Right: Patterns of Popular Support in 1984 and 1996." (with Matthew DeBell and Lee Sigelman). *Social Science Quarterly* 80: 181–192

Wilcox, Clyde, John C. Green, and Mark J. Rozell. 1995. "Faith, Hope, and Conflict: The Christian Right in State Republican Politics." Presented at the annual meeting of the American Sociological Association, Washington, DC.

Wilcox, Clyde, and Ted G. Jelen. 1990. "Evangelicals and Political Tolerance." *American Politics Quarterly* 18:25–46.

Wilcox, Clyde, Ted G. Jelen, and Sharon Linzey. 1991. "Reluctant Warriors: Premillennialism and Politics in the Moral Majority." *Journal for the Scientific Study of Religion* 30:245–258.

———. 1995. "Rethinking the Reasonableness of the Religious Right." *Review of Religious Research* 36:263–276.

Wilcox, Clyde, Mark J. Rozell, and Roland Gunn. 1996. "Religious Coalitions in the New Christian Right." *Social Science Quarterly* 77:543–559.

Wilcox, Clyde, and Robin Wolpert. 2000. "Gay Rights in the Public Sphere: Public Opinion on Gay and Lesbian Equality." In Craig A. Rimmerman, Kenneth D. Wald, and Clyde Wilcox (eds.), *The Politics of Gay Rights.* Chicago: University of Chicago Press.

Williamsburg Charter. 1988. *Surveys of Church-State Attitudes.* Computer data file.

Wills, Garry. 1990. *Under God: Religion and American Politics.* New York: Simon and Schuster.

Wimberly, Ronald C. 1976. "Testing the Civil Religion Hypothesis." *Sociological Analysis* 40:59–62.

Wolfinger, Raymond E., Barbara Kaye Wolfinger, Kenneth Prewitt, and Sheilah Rosenhack. 1969. "America's Radical Right: Politics and Ideology." In R. Schoenberger (ed.), *The American Right Wing*. New York: Holt, Rinehart, and Winston.

Zwier, Robert. 1984. *Born-Again Politics: The New Christian Right in America*. Downer's Grove, IL: Intervarsity Press.

About the Book and Author

They have money, influence, power—and they turn out to vote. They are credited with delivering a significant part of the Republicans' stunning 1994 electoral success, which foreshadowed their status as major players in the elections of 1996 and 2000.

"They" are groups like the Moral Majority, the Christian Coalition, and the religious Right. But are they the greatest threat to liberty since Hitler or the last defenders of religious freedom and family values in America? In this book Clyde Wilcox tells us who they are, what their history has been in twentieth-century American politics, and how they might organize themselves for future political effectiveness. He tackles the sticky political dilemma of the proper role of religious groups in American politics and government while showing how the contemporary religious Right does—and does not—fit into that context.

Clyde Wilcox is professor of government at Georgetown University.

Index